GREAT EXPECTATIONS OF AGING

Peggy Y. Boone, Ph.D.

Growing old is an honor…

(Prov. 16:31)

Dedications

To my children: Eric Wade Boone and Wilma Jean Cook Boone for their devoted counsel and care. And to my departed parents John Wade and Evelyn Yancey.

They were the first to love me on earth.

CONTENTS

FOREWORD

There was a time, in other societies, when age was a virtue synonymous with valued experience and wisdom; something to be revered or esteemed. But, over the generations of this new world, the survival of the fittest was necessary, and age quickly became a liability and a lonely burden. Because we were raised with the belief that only performers were worthy of contributing to a rapidly expanding society, we tend to think of ourselves in that way as we age. However, a new day is coming, and we are here as proof that God's calendar is the only one that counts.

It is difficult to define the condition of "old"; according to the Beatles, it was 64, according to the government it is 65, 90+ according to the actuaries, and 120, 70 or 80 according to the Bible. As a human trait, we are fearful of the designation and avoid connection to the term "old" whenever possible. We instead use such "weasel words" as elderly, seniors, retirees, senior citizens, prime timers, and perennials.

We establish such classifications as:

GI Generation – born between 1901-1924 (lucky ones)

Silent generation (traditionalists) – born between 1925-1942

Boomers – those born between 1943-1964

Generation X – those born between 1965-1979

Millennials – those born between 1980-2000

Generation Z – born between 2001 – 2013 (1)

According to recent research, the average lifespan in developing countries should be 115 years, with a maximum age of 125. (2) AARP tells us that 1 in 4 reach the age of 95. Few people attain that age, even with today's medical advances, technological discoveries, and miracles.

However you determine it, you'll know it when you feel it! My favorite definition, no matter the years attached, is: old is when there is a frequent disconnect between body and brain, and a renewed concern about the condition of the soul.

Some define old as 70-85 and old-old as 86-100. It's not the years but the condition. Humans can be old at 60 and still young at 80. Only our bodies are advancing. The body and the brain do not age equally. The society in which we live and work only considers the condition of the body. The body does require more upkeep to finish strong, but the mind is still on the path that God intended. The spirit in us does not age!

One man described his battle with age: "When I was 19, I looked 14. I did everything I could to look older – like growing a mustache, and wearing fake glasses so that I would be taken more seriously. Then, when I got older, I did everything I could to look younger so that I could still be taken more seriously. Age is just a number, and old is a mindset."

At birth, humans arrive with four common characteristics: naked, bald, dependent, and protesting. At death, they leave with the same four common characteristics: naked, balding, dependent, and protesting. There are other similar characteristics at the birth and re-birth points of human experience. Infants come into the world with all their needs met by their Heavenly Father. As they are "gifted" to their earthly parents, it becomes the parents' responsibility to love and nurture their children as they grow and adapt to the confusion of this world.

Some studies cite the memories in very young children of interactions in heaven before birth and some of them speak of participation in choosing their own earthly parents. In some circles, infants are implored to talk about God before they forget.

Dr. Wayne Dyer records examples of personal recollections from all over the world in his book Memories of Heaven:

> When my son, Daniel, was about two
> years old, he told me that when we

are born, we know everything but as we grow up, we forget. It blew me away so much that I still remember it. – Lesley Timms, West Midlands, United Kingdom.

When my son, Dustin, was around two years of age, we were riding around in the car and he hit himself on the forehead with his hand – kind of like the commercial that states, "I could've had a V8." And he said, "Mama, I'm starting to forget what heaven looks like." Needless to say, it gave me chills. – Sherri Junkins, Greenville, South Carolina. (3)

Perhaps this is why many describe their pending death as "going home."

As the years pass, the knowledge of heaven and the prior relationship with God seems lost. However, as these same children grow older, the enlightened ones begin to connect again with the awareness that they came into the world with a purpose, planned by God. Much time is devoted to an assessment of how closely that purpose is being achieved.

For this notoriously unscientific study, I wanted to discover what happens as we age and how personality and emotional health determines how we face the common challenges. The subjects were recruited from a cross-section of our society: from schools, hospitals, churches, retirement homes, fellow travelers, new acquaintances, and a circle of relatives and friends. I also wanted to find out what the experts have to say about aging. Direct quotes are referenced and cited – ideas and thoughts paraphrased and edited to fit the themes of the author, based on what was heard and seen from the generous people who agreed to be interviewed about their experience with age.

Not every aging person will exhibit these characteristics and those who do will have them in varying degrees. Without a doubt, however. most of us will see ourselves In each chapter.

The book records how it was for the old, how it is for boomers and expectations of how it will be for the millennials and younger people (maybe).

AGING?

ging is a continuous process of change that begins in early adulthood. During middle age, bodily functions begin a gradual decline. However, people do not become elderly at any specific age. Traditionally, age 65 has been designated as the beginning of old age. The reason was based on history, not physical condition: this age is close to the actual retirement age of most people in economically advanced societies.

There are different ways to describe when a person becomes old:

- **The chronological age is based solely on the passage of time. Because chronologic age helps predict many health problems, it has some legal and financial uses.**

- **Biologic age refers to changes in the body that commonly occur as people age. Some people are biologically old at 65, and others not until a decade or more later.**

- **Psychologic age is based on how people act and feel. An 80-year-old who works, plans, looks forward to future events, and particBipates in many activities is considered psyBchologically younger. (4)**

This poem (from the public domain) captures the psychological young.

How Old Are You?

Possibly authored by H. S. Fritsch

Age is a quality of mind.

If you have left your dreams behind.

If hope is cold.

If you no longer look ahead.

If your ambitions' fires are dead –
Then you are old.

But if from life you take the best.

And if in life you keep the jest.

If love you hold;

Peggy Y. Boone, Ph.D.

No matter how the years go by,

No matter how the birthdays fly—

You are not old.

People generally put too much emphasis on age (usually for comparison purposes). The common age question is "How old are you?" That question implies that "old" is a destination: progress on some linear measure that we are flying toward. It is inappropriate when the "old" destination is not the same for each of us. A more appropriate question is: "How many years have you been on earth?" or "How many years have you completed?" We forget that birthdays signify completed years, not future years. To understand that concept, we must start with children. A first birthday means that a child has completed one year on earth; a 50th birthday

signifies that an individual has been on earth for 50 years, and is working on 51. I know, it is easier to ask, "How old are you?" as it's quicker and more expected. But some changes must start with us.

Our ancestors may have wrestled with age concepts when they wrote of a child being considered a man at twelve (Jesus in the temple) and the Jewish custom that a child becomes an adult (the age of accountability) at the age of thirteen. Scripture does not solve the confusion. It does, however, tell us that the age when a child can distinguish right from wrong and become capable of choosing Christ likely varies from child to child. A sense of guilt and conviction of sin starts to develop in the pre-adolescent years. Only the Lord knows when each child reaches that point. This is a great comfort to parents who have lost a young child.

"...I will go to him, but he will not return to me." King David on the death of his first son with Bathsheba. (2 Samuel 12:22).

Humans may be confused about age, but the Lord isn't. Each of us has a preconceived appointment as to when, where, and how we will leave this world.

Besides graying hair, other fascinating phenomena of aging are the disappearance of fingerprints and the change in eye color.

An 89-year-old woman shared:

"I don't have fingerprints anymore. When I went to renew my license, they could not complete the application because they could not find my fingerprints. After three trips on different days, I gave up. Does that

mean I cannot prove my citizenship

and verify my identity? That makes

me feel different and insignificant."

Studies about the 1-2 percent of elders who lose their fingerprints indicate that the prints are not really gone. They were formed as one of the last developments in the womb and are permanent throughout life. Our means of scanning the fingertips is causing the lack of proof that they still exist.

For the aging, as for all adults, fingerprints do remain the same for a lifetime. However, skin condition changes as we grow older. The skin gradually loses elasticity and becomes drier. This is thought to be caused by a decrease in collagen. There are also other possible medical conditions, typical of age, such as arthritis, which can hinder the acquisition of distinct fingerprints.

The current live-scan touch-based scanners cannot produce an image of sufficient quality to compare the prints to previous ones for identification. The scanners cannot read the drier size, depth of firmness, and ridge width of the fingerprints. In this age of expanding technology, we should do better.

A change in eye color occurs in up to 15 percent of all Caucasian people throughout their lifetime. Several factors can contribute to eyes becoming darker or lighter over time:

- emotion – anger, happiness, sadness, crying

- sun exposure – melanin in the eye is influenced by the sun's rays

- diet – nuts, onions, fish, honey and spinach all have the potential to change eye color

- trauma to the eye (5)

A number of the elderly people interviewed spoke of their eye color "fading" as the acuity worsens.

~ 9 ~

My heart pounds, my strength fails me; even the light has gone from my eyes.

(Psalm 38:10).

HAPPINESS

As you advance in age, you can expect to be happier than you have ever been before. By the age of 80, about 55 percent of Americans say they feel joyful and content, versus 31 percent at age 20. (6)

Dartmouth College economist David Blanchflower put it simply: people, in general, hit high levels of happiness in their early 20s, low levels in middle age (around age 47), and then start seeing a steady increase in joy from that point. He describes a U-curve as we move through the later years. The typical person grows steadily happier as each year passes. (7)

We shouldn't be surprised at this conclusion when we have always had the secret of contentment from St. Paul: *"I have learned the secret of being content in any and every situation..." (Phil. 4:12)*

However, it seems that the basis for contentment is not the same for all of us. Some cannot wait to retire when hobbies or travel is the focus. Others feel content to work until they drop to see tangible production from their efforts. Which is right? Neither. Joy is where your individual DNA leads.

Many of us desire to find out where we came from and what our ancestors did. Numerous companies are ready to help with that search, (for a fee). We wish we had asked more questions of our parents and grandparents about what they knew. We wish to have taken the time to listen to their memories. Searching for lost or unknown relatives takes an urgent purpose to elicit their memories that we might add to ours.

The following was overheard at a recent "high society" party:

> "My ancestry goes back to Alexander the Great," said Christine. She then turned to Miriam and asked, "How far back does your family go?" "I don't know," replied Miriam, "All of our records were lost in the flood."(8)

We may spend more time on finding out where we came from than on where we are going next!

Another phenomenon that we may suffer is a need to "live on the land." Human beings haven't changed much in 4,000 years. The desire for land still crops up with surprising emotional issues. At the age of around 55 or 60, as the first ideas of retirement surface, we start thinking of parcels of isolated land to own – possess, not necessarily work, just to build on and call their own. It is particularly enticing if that land could be a place previously owned by family members. As one beneficiary described the feeling about family land:

"If there is no family to listen, will the leaves fall? What if no one recognizes the sighing, whispering trees as they talk? After centuries of nurture, can the land stand separation and detachment from the original caretakers? My forefathers walked and talked on this land. They lived on, prayed for, and revered this land. What will happen if there is no one to treasure the awakening of spring? Or value a wide-eyed fawn trembling as it steps out beside its proud mother? I don't want to be accused as the one that abandons the land. My ancestors are depending on me."

Today, no one seems to purchase land for future financial benefits. Real estate agents tell about the majority of older customers who are not interested in the acceleration of wealth from the land, but the notion of living on it for a short time and leaving family land for their survivors. There is a pioneer spirit in us all!

So, it seems that we all have different retirement plans. But, John Piper says in Rethinking Retirement – For the Glory of God, "…knowing that we have an infinitely satisfying and everlasting inheritance in God just over the horizon of life makes us zealous in our few remaining years to spend ourselves in the sacrifices of love, not the accumulation of comforts." (9)

Happiness does not just occur; it has to be worked on. Oprah Winfrey says, "Every day brings a chance for you to draw a breath, kick off your

shoes, and dance." If you start the day with gratitude and the expectation of being happy and seeking
it in others, you will find happiness in abundance.

"I worked for God all of my life
and I know I will soon be dancing
in Heaven. But I wish I had danced
more during my time on earth".

– Mother Teresa

ANXIETY

Anxiety is a "weasel word" for fear: fear of failure, fear of rejection, fear of loss, fear of violence, fear of death. Hundreds of other fears hide in these categories which guarantee that every one of us at one time will suffer from anxiety.

Most fears never materialize. They are projections into the future where bad things may, will, or could happen. Circumstances and possibilities will change as you ruminate on the problem. Anxious people are worriers. They tend to hold on to problems that are already gone. They question their own decisions and project the impact of those decisions upon others.

Anxiety feeds anxiety, and misery loves company. Two anxious people together spell disaster. What one can visualize, the other can hypothesize. The anxiety can be brought on by others, or by your own thoughts of the worst-case scenario. Anxiety can be habit-forming; it keeps our brain busy with stale possibilities while there are new real problems to be solved. Indecision and procrastination may cause long-term anxiety and impulsive actions.

Anxiety may be treated by a professional or managed by yourself. But you must first search for the source of the fear causing the anxiety.

It may be necessary to stir memories as far back as kindergarten when you were the only one in the class that couldn't cut along the lines or the time you had to stay after school with another student to help you learn to carry in subtraction. Or you might remember comparing your used ball gown to the most beautiful one at the seventh-grade dance; relive when your old dog stopped breathing; or when the flood in your parent's home required the family to live in a hotel for five weeks as repairs were done. Remember the experience of the entire family – in one hotel room! Or recall when one of your parents expressed profound disappointment in you.

As you do this search you will find that all these events can be posted under the categories listed above: failure, rejection, loss, violence, and death.

At the finish, look at your records and see how many times you were anxious but did what you needed to do and got through it. Why then do you doubt that you can get through whatever is caus-ing you anxiety today? You are a master at handling whatever may come – so chill out! As you get older, the expectation of others is that you are more set-tled, and not as easily distressed about things. It is true that you are anxious about fewer things, but anxiety about specific things is just as intense as it has always been. Anxiety can still develop into anger quickly. Deliberate slow thinking engages the wisdom and thoughtful delay of the appropriate response to deal with anger and other disorders of impulse control.

Anxiety for someone else is even more challeng-ing than for ourselves. It is harder mainly because you cannot predict how the person will react or if they even know they should be anxious. If they do not per-ceive a problem, they will not be anxious to solve it!

If we are lucky enough to become grandparents, our "anxiety pool" expands. There are more loved ones to worry about, and more strangers to evaluate as new family members.

Basically, anxiety is a fear of losing control. As you grow older, there is a sense that you have less power to exert change to avoid calamity in the lives of those you love. There is less time to work on changing things. You must realize that you are or were never in control. Only God controls what happens to all of us, and some of that might be hard and even frightening at times. However, remember you are only responsible for your own behavior in dealing with the anxiety caused by stressful situations.

Some suggestions for dealing with anxiety attacks are:

Commit to taking time away from work or your regular setting.

Practice deep abdominal breathing. Breathe deeply and slowly through your nose, deliberately taking the air down to your abdomen, and then breathe out slowly through pursed lips.

Replace negative thoughts with positive ones. Talk to yourself about the reasonability of your fear. Exposure to negative stereotypes about aging makes some older people perform badly on memory tests – meeting that negative expectation.

Picture yourself successfully facing and conquering a specific fear.

Start the day right with breakfast and continue with frequent small meals throughout the day. Eat your last meal prior to 6:00 pm.

Reduce alcohol and nicotine. Also reduce caffeine, tea, cola, and chocolate consumption.

Exercise is a natural stress and anxiety reliever. Aim for at least 30 minutes of aerobic exercise on most days.

A lack of sleep can exacerbate anxious thoughts and feelings, try to get 7 to 9 hours of quality sleep a night.

A recent study found that only 10 minutes with a furry friend will relieve stress by 9 percent. (10)

When you experience anxiety, write down your worries. Writing down is harder work than simply thinking, so your negative thoughts are likely to lessen - plus, you have a record of your worry which you can review over and over if needed. Check off, when you have already settled that!

Accept uncertainty and do not require immediate solutions to life's problems. Ask for help from the One who is in charge of everything then wait.

In severe anxiety cases consider:

1. If others are involved, sever the association for a while.

2. Change location. Find a place to cool off and rethink the problem.

3. **If possible, consider an actual or mental place that resembles the one that Patrick O'Leary (11) describes:**

No One Knows It But Me

There's a place I travel when I want to roam, and nobody knows it but me. The roads don't go there and the signs stay home, and nobody knows it but me. It's far, far away and way, way afar. It's over the moon and the sea, and wherever you're going that's where you are, and no one knows it but me.

When practiced regularly, prayer, and relaxation techniques such as mindfulness (attention to your present thoughts and feelings), meditation, progressive muscle relaxation, music, and deep breathing can reduce anxiety symptoms and increase feelings of emotional well-being.

Above all, avoid worry. Worrying or living an anxious life is unfaithful, unproductive and wrong:

it is unfaithful because of our Father,

it is wrong because of our faith,

it is unwise because of the mystery of our future.

"Therefore, I tell you, do not worry about your life..." Matthew 6:25.

"Cast all your anxiety on Him because He cares for you." 2 Peter 7.

LONELINESS

At some time in your life, you will probably be alone, by choice or incident. No one cares where you are and no one expects you. You are free to wander, drink as you want, eat when hungry, and sleep where you drop. But you may experience profound emotional loneliness – loneliness for the times that used to be and the people who shared them with you. The ARRP Magazine of December 2019 states that some researchers believe the intensely personal experience of rejection, disconnection, and longing produces pain as real as any caused by a physical injury, one that has little to do with living arrangements or social networks.

There is no preparation for being totally alone. Even before birth, in the womb, you were not alone but were being formed by God (Psalm 39:13) and nourished by your mother. God has not left you since.

Dr. David Jeremiah (12) says that there is a fundamental emptiness in every human being that can only be filled by the presence of God Himself. Therefore, we are never, never, ever totally alone.

There is a difference between the feeling of being lonely and the state of loneliness. The feeling of being lonely is a temporary condition usually self-induced and eventually resolved. The state of perpetual loneliness is to be a long-term victim of perceived abandonment and social failure.

Across the globe, the incidence of people living alone is 40-60%. There is a 32% increased risk of early death for those living alone, according to a study of 3.4 million people. (13) Researchers are scurrying to find a solution to the epidemic of loneliness that is costing this country millions of dollars in health care and the loss of many valuable people through suicide.

Not all loneliness victims are elders; young people too cite loneliness as a perceived problem. There are many married victims, living with their spouses, who report pervasive loneliness. Teenagers especially feel that the pain of loneliness is theirs alone. One may exist in a noisy, loveable family but experience extreme loneliness. Illness too is a lonely island. There is no loneliness like affliction; there is only isolation and despair.

Reasons for the increase in people living alone are varied: longer life spans, later marriages, higher divorce rates, lower birth rates, and pessimism regarding the motivation and actions of other people.

Chronically lonely people approach social interactions looking for evidence that others are hypocritical and phony. And of course, they find that evidence. Others see home as a refuge as they ruminate on the actions of others.

Guy Winch, in Psychology Today states that it is not the number or proximity of our social relationships that matters, but the internal sense of their quality and depth. As humans, we need relationships that reflect common values and experiences. (14) We also need to work to broaden our innate values and experiences. We all need a witness to our lives and people to look after. That witness can be

Jesus and in His word, He tells us to seek out cultur-ally different people to love.

It is difficult to gauge the depth of loneliness. It is a subjective, self-reported moving target. Most of the information we give about our relationships comes from nonverbal clues, our words simply do not reveal the truth behind our actions. If you do experience persistent and profound loneliness, you may see the state as a result of your failures. These thoughts may make it difficult to admit to others.

There are extreme and conflicting views about being alone and the importance of relationships. In Silent Spring, Rachel Carson says "In nature, nothing exists alone." "Loneliness and the feeling of being unloved is the most terrible poverty. – Mother Teresa.

Jennifer Pharr Davis (speaker, author, hiker, and entrepreneur), values solitude. "Through spending time by myself on the trail, I learned what made me laugh when no one else was around and what made me cry when there was no hope of sympathy. It allowed me to grieve because no one tried to fix it. It's a place where you can truly let it out and be in the moment."

While a 90-year-old woman expresses a different view: "There is no one who shares my memories about how it was. I am afraid that my life doesn't matter anymore." She expressed a yearning – not just for the past but for the passage of time and for the cruel irreversibility of it. (15)

All lives matter! Until God calls you home, seek companionship and enjoy relationships with others as you pursue specific goals for your temporary earthly sojourn.

GOALS

OK, you are thinking of retirement or have taken the plunge. You no longer have to get up at 5 AM to get to an unfulfilling job. Oh! you don't have to get up at all unless you want to. You can sit up all night and watch TV or surf the web, then sleep all day if it suits you. What luxury! What freedom!

Building birdhouses is a possibility, but soon your relatives and friends are equipped to house all the bird types in the country. Learning new skills is another possibility. Local colleges have entry courses – some are even free. And, gray-haired graduates are encountered more and more at the university level. But with what direction? The direction that your job provided (hello!) In many ways that job gave you an obtainable goal every day, month, and year that you were employed. It may have been the same goal every day, but it was a goal provided by your employer and was a target for the distant future.

Now it is all up to you, this daunting task. It is necessary to set goals, otherwise we let life just happen to us, stumbling along without a plan and squandering the days and years we live. As Yogi Berra, the New York Yankees catcher and philosopher said: "If you don't know where you're going, you'll end up someplace else."

One of the amazing things we have been given as humans is the unquenchable desire to have dreams of a better life and the ability to establish and set goals to live out these dreams. (16)

To set your new goals, you must start and end with paperwork.

1. Take an interest inventory, some are free on the Internet.

2. List your current talents, skills, dreams, and financial means.

    Your dreams aren't what you already have or past efforts that failed, but what you now want. Your dreams are there; they may live right on the surface of your heart and mind, or they may be buried deep as a foolish impossibility.

3. Consider how chasing your dreams will affect the lives of others, particularly family members. Discover what you need to add to

your skills given your interests and capabilities. Pray that your dreams are approved by God.

4. Establish an attainable goal that you can tackle in small steps. Write it down and post it where it is visible every day. The mere act of writing the goal makes it more possible. You cannot forget it, except on purpose.

5. Develop a reasonable timeline for each step toward that goal, and cross off each step as you accomplish it. No pressure, it is your plan.

6. Share your plan with someone you trust who will hold you accountable for the process. Do not let them evaluate the goal; it belongs to you.

7. Review your plan regularly for progress and motivation. Do not be discouraged if there is no progress for that review.

8. Adjust your plan for unforeseen problems as needed, but stay true to plan.

9. Celebrate each small or large success along the way.

10. Recognize that your goal may never be completely realized, but the effort will be worth it. It will establish a pattern for your next endeavor and will provide an example for others.

That list of how to set goals is much like the 10 valuable rules for making fundamental changes in behavior – and even personality – at any age, as cited in the January/February/2018 issue of Psychology Today:

- Don't beat yourself up for your problem; it serves a purpose.

- Acknowledge the fear of failing to meet a wanted goal.

- List the pros and cons of changing and inventory all the forces working for and against change.

- Prepare in advance ways to counter feelings of frustration and discouragement.

- Stay attuned to the dream; give yourself regular reminders.

- Align your thoughts, feelings, and behaviors with your goal.

- **Engage in any activity that boosts faith in yourself.**

- **Keep friends around; they lift your mood.**

- **Accept the discomfort of uncertainty that change brings, it's only temporary.**

My friend Joyce Rice, author and action speaker, exclaims that whether setting a goal or making a change in behavior or personality, it's your action plan. So, Think it, Work it, Do it! (17)

SLEEP

You can expect sleeping problems as you age. Up to 50% of people over the age of 70 have trouble falling asleep and staying asleep. Sleep problems vary and become more common as we age. Millions are spent yearly on sleep aids: pills and apparatuses, usually to no avail.

Scientists believe that seven hours of sleep is required for the body to replenish our brains so that we can function while awake. Less than six hours cause severe lapses in the brain. Lost sleep affects our decision-making abilities and the interpretation of new information.

Despite the popular view that in sleep we are working on unfinished business from the day, the brain is always working on new information. The waking brain is charged with collecting information, and the sleeping brain for consolidating that information. At night we switch from recording experiences to editing and discarding the unimportant collected items. (18) While that vital work is underway, most of us are waking up to frequent bathroom trips.

There is a universal theory that the aged use small increments of sleep during the day that make up for the hours of interrupted sleep at night. Actually, the daytime short intervals of sleep are not subtracted minutes from night sleep but are supplemental minutes for the few who can snatch naps during the day. Maybe the aging requires more sleep because our brains work slowly as they examine and file the information we need. However, even the young often can't find the file!

God gave us an efficient work-sleep pattern. Work while there is light and sleep in the dark. He made us such that we keep in sync with the sun. This rhythm served man for eons; then, he gave man electric lights and the system alignment became confused. We reasoned that production would be greater if we slept shorter hours. As Robert Frost protested: "But I have promises to keep and miles to go before I sleep."

Thomas Edison, who gave us light bulbs, said that "sleep is an absurdity, a bad habit." He believed we'd eventually dispense with it entirely. He may be right!

According to the August 2018 National Geographic, technological advances have served to give us not only red incandescent light but blue light. Blue light, previously thought to be soothing and sleep-inducing, has recently been found to be the most disturbing to sleep. Most of our cell phones, smart TVs, tablets, and other LED-illuminated screens emit blue, bright light which prevents melatonin release and interrupts our sleep cycle.

As our eyesight changes due to advancing years, red-green is the first color to fade. To compensate, we find ourselves interpreting traffic lights by position rather than color. When you renew your driver's license you may be tested on distinguishing the red and green traffic lights. We should worry that signs of danger everywhere may be missed because of this fading. The blue-yellow light stays with us longer, which sometimes confuses our brains and causes insomnia.

Everything we learn about sleep reinforces its importance to our mental and physical health.

Our sleep-wake pattern is a central feature of human biology, and also a primary target of our conversation. In our restless, floodlit society, we often think of sleep as an opponent, depriving us of productivity and play, and even a sense of guilt if uncontrolled.

Sunlight exposure, diet, and physical activity have a big impact on the quality of our sleep. All activities we like to avoid at any age!

Scientists also tell us that we are sexually stimulated repeatedly during sleep (men and women). During the REM (deepest) period of sleep, there is an engorgement of sexual organs and virtually all vivid dreaming takes place there. What might this be doing to the birth rate?

But what else is going on in our brain while asleep? Dreams occupy a portion of the activity of the sleeping brain. Dr. Elizabeth Murphy, psychologist, author and speaker, describes the process of dreaming:

> Each individual is driven by their conscious side and their unconscious side. In consciousness, we use words to understand and explain people and events. In the unconscious, we process these events in a non-verbal and visual way. The unconscious uses symbols to guide us and these symbols are expressed in dreams. Our dreams may not "make sense" because we do not know how to interpret all the symbols but the dream has a specific purpose to help us grow, develop, and resolve old conflicts. Even if we do not remember

dreams or cannot make sense of dreams, the energy of the dream is there to help us.

Researchers tell us that the top 12 typical dream themes are:

1. being chased

2. sexual experiences

3. school, teachers, studying, failing an exam

4. falling

5. being late or on the verge of being late

6. flying through the air

7. trying repeatedly to do something

8. frozen with fright

9. being physically attacked

10. person now dead as alive; person alive now dead

11. vividly sensing a presence in the room

12. being a child again

(19)

Two other common themes are: teeth falling out and losing the way home.

But some dreams seem not to have a theme at all. One of my infrequent dreams, the meaning of which has alluded me for 12 years, is the following:

Jerusalem hotel, 2012

I was descending a dark and steep staircase in some sort of refuse dump lined with horizontally divided opaque plastic sheets hanging on a long clothesline. I spied the corner of a beautiful golden crocheted table-cloth sparkling on the ground on the other side of the plastic divider. I wanted it. I looked further up the stairs and saw an alcove in the wall where I had seen a long-handled hoe left there by a gardener. I took the hoe back down the stairs and raked the cloth toward me. Just as I grabbed the tablecloth, something or someone I couldn't see grabbed the other end of it. We struggled back and forth to keep it until I heard a loud tear and thump. The tablecloth was destroyed and I quickly forgot the strange episode.

Later, I sat with my group around a table eating and drinking, and saw a tall woman in white standing at the entrance to the staircase.

She beckoned me. She was lovely and serene-looking. She told me that her son had an injured hand and she was afraid that his nerves were damaged; he needed help and that I should give her money to take him to a doctor. I told her that I was a doctor and to let me see his hand. I found that it was an old, nearly healed wound and suggested that we call the tourist police to settle the matter. She and her son retreated.

What was this very detailed dream sent to teach me: pride, coveting, envy, persistence, discrimination, arrogance, suspicion, deception, a threat? And, why has it stayed with me so long? I relate this dream to emphasize that some dreams instruct and potentially help us and others just confuse us. But, trying to discern the difference is worth the effort.

We have no control over dreams and little memory of most of them. Several strange phenomena of dreams are experiencing the same dream over and over again and having a dream pick up where it left off the night before. That must be an important dream!

We do, however, have a measure of control over how to have a more restful sleep:

<u>Set a schedule</u>. Establish a bedtime and keep it!

<u>Upgrade your bedroom</u> with fresh pillows, replace a worn-out mattress, remove the TV from the room and if possible keep a low volume of soothing music playing.

<u>Change the lighting</u>. Use no artificial lighting whatsoever. (If you wake in the middle of the night do not reach for the cell phone. That light will reset your internal clock for a wake-up at the same time the next night.)

Many disparities exist in the night as in the day. The wealthy sleep better than the poor and whites sleep better than people of color. Women sleep more than men but have more interrupted sleep. Men are more satisfied with their sleep (probably because the woman is programmed to guard his sleep and that of the children). There is also an age gap. Young adults sleep better and sleep more. Experts tell us that if you expect to be able to sleep like you did when you were young, you're going to be disappointed.

We are all living with the consequences of sleep deprivation. We should have known – Soloman told us centuries ago in Psalm 127:

" In vain you rise early and stay up late, toiling for food to eat – but He grants sleep for those he loves."

A well-spent day brings happy sleep, so a life well-spent brings a happy death.

(Leonardo da Vinci)

DEATH

We will all die. Although we don't know when our life will expire, we know that it will, and soon. We just hope it won't hurt and won't leave our loved ones without hope that they will see us again. One of the older ladies interviewed said, "I try really hard not to think of it." As hard as the dear lady tried, I doubt she was successful, for we all have those thoughts hardwired in our brains.

In the New Testament (James 4:14) human life is described as a vapor that appears for a little time and then vanishes away. David in Psalm 90:12 implores God to teach us to number our days so that we may get a heart of wisdom. Numbering days does not dwell on how many are gone and how many may be ahead, but on making the most of every day you are given. Preparing for death is one of the tasks we must accomplish while we have the breath to do so.

Katy Butler in The Art of Dying Well, tells us that only seven percent of us will die suddenly, as we all wish. Three-quarters of Americans still hope to die at home, fewer than a third of us do so, and the rest die in hospitals, nursing homes, and other institutions. Nearly a third spend time in an intensive care unit in the month before, and 27 percent of Americans die in an ICU. She writes that the fortunate 25 percent who prepare through their own efforts, and the support of a loving community, may not need much assistance until close to the very end of life.

Her guiding principles of preparation are:

- **Have a vision of a "high-quality of life". What steps do you need to take to start living it today?**

- **Start with what requires the most of you and the least of medicine.**

- **Five-cent solutions will usually do more for your well-being than a single "silver bullet" cure. The miracle drugs of later life are water, exercise, and community.**

- **An ounce of prevention beats a pound of cure.**

- **Focus on staying as functional as possible, and let longevity take care of itself.**

- **Now is the time to take inventory, build reserves, and assess what needs shoring up.**

- **The biggest threats to your continuing independence will be: cognitive impairment, a simple fall, or a degenerative but preventable health condition. (20)**

People's fears of death fall into four major categories:

1. pain – fear of the processes of the body;

2. the unknown – what, if anything, happens after death;

3. loss of control;

4. a life not fully lived. (21)

If fear of dying is the final loss of control, take control while you are able. Change what needs to be changed to push the eventuality of death further away.

Very few of us are considered wealthy. However, most of us tend to hoard our money to fund a future health crisis or long-term old-age care. We may be our worst enemy in doing so. Either event will cost much more than we could ever save.

According to a CBS News posting in 2018, Americans aged 65 and older are declaring bankruptcy at an alarming rate. Why is this happening?

- Many of them are trying to rely on 401(k) plans which were underfunded (they didn't save enough). Many of them don't have pensions.

- Out-of-pocket medical expenses are going through the roof.

- Their debt load is far too high, including large mortgage balances. The average American household pays $900 per year in credit card interest.

- **They are co-signing student loans for their kids and grandkids and getting stuck with the bill.**

- **They continue to support the adult kids.**

- **Emergency savings accounts get wiped out by healthcare expenses.**

- **Some realize they should have delayed their retirement and continued working.**

- **Some may need to delay starting Social Security until they at least reach their "full retirement age."**

Based on the above information, a more sensible way to guarantee care for ourselves is to rid ourselves of that stash of money we have so that we will qualify for Medicaid and Social Security to care for us long-term. We are allowed to gift $18,000.00 a year to any person without them having to pay taxes on it.

For instance, if you have four children and ten grandchildren, you can gift them a total of $252,000. per year. Starting this distribution early enough, you can probably qualify for help as soon as you need it. Early is the watchword. You cannot dump your savings into an account for your children after you require care from Medicaid or other assistance agencies.

All of us want to cause our loved ones the least amount of indecision and grief.

Four imperative tasks of preparation:

1. Financial – purchase an HMO or Medicare Advantage plan, give money away.

2. Will – keep your will current, even if you have to attach codicils to all copies if you make changes. Leave multiple copies.

3. Relocate if necessary to live as close to relatives or friends as possible.

4. Leave clear and written funeral instructions. Your wishes may not be carried out, but there will be a record of how you wanted to say goodbye.

It is hard to discuss death without recalling the worldwide phenomena of near-death experiences (NDE) so prevalent in this age. These accounts are particularly precious to me since my youngest son experienced an NDE during heart surgery.

He first described to me his experience when he was seventeen. He shared that he had been to the light. He said that he had been on a table and the doctors were working on him when he became aware that he was above them observing. He said that he had this out-of-body experience several times before during his many surgeries. However, this time was different because an extremely bright light appeared and it began drawing him to it. The light became brighter and brighter until it was all around him – until he and the light were one. He found himself in a place so beautiful that there were no words to describe it. He only wanted to be there – to stay there. He just knew that he was in the presence of God and that God was with him, holding him. God was all around him and he was united with God.

He said that he was aware that by staying in this place he would not have any more pain and he would always be warm. He also knew that he would never be afraid, lonely, sad, or hurt ever again. He told me that although no words were spoken there, he knew everything about everything all at once. He knew that there he would be forever loved, happy, warm, accepted, and whole. He said that he gradually knew that he would eventually return to this heavenly place but now he was coming back to this life. Instantly, he was in his body with the doctors in the room with the machines, the pain, and the cold. After the surgery, the doctors reported to us that they had lost him for a little while.

John Burke has written two books that trace NDE accounts from all over the world, as experienced by Christians, Muslims, Buddhists, Hindus, and people of a host of other faiths, and even those with no faith at all. Although related in various languages, all have common episodes during the event. (22)

My son did not share his story with many people - afraid that they would ridicule him. However, each time he shared with a trusted family member and friend, he cried as he described heaven and his unwilling return to earth. I trust that the NDE that he experienced gave him comfort years later when he didn't come back.

LOSS

One of the tasks of growing older is to prepare for dying (not our own, that job belongs to the Lord). But as we age, we are destined to lose more and more of our loved ones, friends, and acquaintances. A favorite uncle voiced: "Everyone I know is dying." They seem to leave the earth without warning: no matter how old, how ill, or how tragic an event.

Shock precedes a comparison to our own mortality. Recall of the last communication or encounter with the departed is shared liberally with others. The premonition of anticipatory doom is often part of the hindsight which heightens the feeling of involvement or responsibility for prevention of the death in some way. Eventually, we think of the bereaved family and other friends who are dealing with the same grief and sorrow. We become a member of a club which no one wants to join. Funerals will become an element of social life, as we mingle with the same people regularly

> Grief – acute hurt, disbelief, wishing
> it hadn't happened.

> Sorrow – grief and guilt that you
> failed in some way.

Since Kubler-Ross wrote her landmark book in 1969, there has been an acceptance of the "truth" that grief and/or sorrow has a recognizable and predictable sequence, stages which the bereaved individual passes through like rooms in a large and painful house, coming out on the other side into sort of a peaceful garden of acceptance. (23) Other experts in the field disagree with this sequenced recovery. Most agree that there is no sequence at all and usually no recovery. Even the term "stage" implies a progression toward an end.

There are however other sequence expectations. Parents are supposed to die before their children. Old-old people are expected to be killed by some irreversible and advancing malady. Lifestyles such as smoking, drinking, overweight, or poor eating habits set the stage for death at an early age. And of course, overwhelming mental problems lead many individuals of all ages to suicide.

According to the Suicide Data and Statistics charts, suicide is one of the leading causes of death in the United States. Suicide rates increased by 37% between 2000-2018 and have been rising every year since, except for the 2018-2020 interval (Covid?) Deaths by suicide increased 2.6% from 2021 to 2022, according to the last report available. (24)

Those statistics point to one suicide death every 11 minutes. The typical suicide victim in the US is a white male over 65 years of age, using a firearm. The suicide rate among males in 2021 was approximately four times higher than the rate among females. Males make up 50% of the population but nearly 80% of suicides. People 85 and older have the highest rates of suicide of all. It is debatable whether suicide is cowardice or heroic.

We usually use the terms grief, sorrow, and mourning interchangeably. However, there is a difference. Grief is considered a more immediate intense feeling of suffering. Sorrow is a long-term unhappiness that can last a lifetime. Both grieving and sorrow are internal feelings about the loss.

Mourning is an external public display of grief for the loss such as the funeral, black clothing, receptions, memorials, etc.

These are not steps to be taken but surges that suddenly occur or increase without warning. In Our Walk with Elephants (25), 18 mothers share their stories of the death of their adult children. Little difference was expressed in the intensity of grief and sorrow from two months to 35 years after the loss.

We can't avoid losing people who are part of our identity and without them, we may never be the same. You may go from being a "wife" or "husband" to a "widow" or "widower." You may go from being a "parent" to a "survivor parent." The way you and the way society defines you has changed. There comes a point when you do have to accept that life is about loss. You're going to lose people you love. You're going to lose your career. Your body is going to degrade. If you're unwilling to accept that reality when it happens, it's going to be devastating. But we can prepare for the eventual losses and recognize them as God's plan for our departed and our own lives as well.

Grief has always been a difficult emotion in America, in a culture focused on happiness and positivity. Although loss is universal, grief has always been individualized. That seems to be slowly changing. Talking openly about death is not the taboo subject that our parents grew up avoiding.

For instance, there are a growing number of "Death Cafes" all over the world. That is a circle of strangers who attend a free-form discussion group that centers around the topic of death. Participants drink coffee and tea, eat cookies, and share their experiences with death and the common and unique fears that linger.

The website describing the objective of a Death Café is: "The group is to increase awareness of death to help people make the most of their (finite) lives. A death café is a group-directed discussion of death with no agenda, objectives, or themes. It is a discussion group rather than a grief support or counseling session." There are no leaders, just moderators without formal qualifications, just good listening skills and enthusiasm for talking about death and dying.

A particularly vulnerable group to long-term grief and sorrow is the survivor of a spouse when the marriage has lasted a great number of years. The survivor is suddenly 'on their own" for the first time since achieving adulthood. The following are typical questions faced by widows and widowers:

fear	finances
aloneness	embarrassment
Intimacy	disappointment

uncovered secrets/anger   unfinished business

change in kids   responsibility

The number one need of grieving, sorrowing and mourning involves confronting the reality that someone you care about will never physically come back into your life again. Others try to comfort you by "he's/she's in a better place," while you struggle to maintain the place they are needed here.

We must develop a new self-identity, internally and externally. Death requires you to take on new roles previously filled by the person who has died. You confront your changed identity every time you do something that used to be the job of the person who is gone and you have no idea how to accomplish the task. You must learn new skills that you always relied on the absent one to possess. This can be very hard work and can leave you feeling angry and drained. Even though you know better, you fluctuate from being angry at the deceased and questioning the fairness of God.

Survivor spouses must use a new vocabulary. There is no longer a "we "or "us", just a "me" and "I." There are clothes, checks, bills and property to be explained as the separation of a "unit" becomes a "single." As a single, is the survivor still a member of the family? Who owns his/her mother's things? Even the mind's calendar changes to begin life on the day of the death.

Jesus promised: "Blessed are those who mourn, for they will be comforted." Matthew 5:4. He didn't say when, how, or where but it is a fact that can be relied upon.

DECLINING HEALTH

This chapter on health is not to reiterate the illnesses, fine doctors, and new medications that may determine how long we live. We know that indulgence in red meat, salt, and sugar will injure our bodies. We know that most illnesses are the result of inflammation. We know all that! And, if we don't know it, our friends will see that we do (health is a number one conversation topic).

Rather, this information is to make you think about what you think about aging. Are you for it or do you fight it? Are you supportive of the process or afraid of it? Or, do you believe, as philosopher Arthur Schopenhauer did: "Life could be compared to embroidery of which we see the right side during the first half of life, but the back in the latter half? This back side is less scintillating but more instructive; it reveals the inter-patterning of the threads." (26)

Do you want to live to 100? Most would answer yes if their physical and mental health remained relatively good. The Bible tells us that "the length of our days is seventy years or eighty if we have the strength..." Psalm 90:10. If you are reading this and are over 70, you are one of the few who have the strength to live longer even if "... the span is but trouble and sorrow for they quickly pass, and we fly away." God is giving you an extension of time to get right with Him.

More magazine articles and books are currently being written on the aged than ever before, probably because more people are living longer and richer lives. They are more likely to have experiences that warrant stories. People of age have become a financial, social, and political force to be reckoned with, but also a complex care requirement. In an urban area, it is hard to drive a block without seeing an assistive living, skilled nursing, or memory care facility, testifying to the number of older people who need such help. As baby boomers age, there will be a dramatic increase in the 70-85 population.

The June 2022 AARP Bulletin reported a survey in which 80% of 60 to 69-year-olds would be at least somewhat likely to take a pill that could extend their life by 10 years. Even 70% of 80+ year-olds said they would be somewhat likely take the pill. Only 40-59-year-olds rated their health less than very good or excellent. This survey and others indicate most aging individuals feel good about their status in life and look forward to any extension possible.

The population of the earth is around 7.8 billion today. Billions are hard to manage, but if you condensed 7.8 billion into 100 persons and then into various percentage statistics, you will find it much easier! Out of the 100, 66 died between the ages of 15-64. Among 100 persons in the world today, only 8 can live or exceed the age of 65. If you are over 65 years old, be content and grateful. Cherish life, grasp the moment. You did not leave this world before the 92 persons who have gone before you. You are already the blessed among mankind. Take good care of your own health. Cherish every remaining moment. (27)

Listen to your body – if it tells you that you need a nap – take one, everything else can wait. If your body is hungry – eat, even if it is not mealtime – and if not hungry, don't eat – you can sit at the table and sip water! Ignore the comments of others, it's your body that is in charge and it is trying to serve you longer.

The average life expectancy has increased a lot in the past century, but the maximum life span has increased little. According to the Guinness World Records, the longest-living person whose dates of birth and death were verified was a French woman who lived to 122. The oldest male lifespan has only been verified as 116 by a Japanese man. There are no reports of what condition these individuals were in during the last years.

Reduction of infant mortality has accounted for most of the increased average life span longevity of today, but since 1960, mortality rates among those over 80 years have decreased by about 1.5% per year. (28) This seems entirely due to medical and public health efforts, rising standards of living, better education, healthier nutrition, and healthy lifestyles.

Currently, studies are being done to ascertain if restricting calories or the ability to repair damaged DNA would further increase our lifespan. By casual observation, we can see that the restriction of calories might not result in longer life but would surely result in more attractive, healthier and happier years.

Do our efforts to increase our number of years negate God's plan for our lifespan? Maybe our efforts should only be to make our 70 or 80 years more independent, healthy, and pleasurable. The millions spent on research for expanding the end of life might be more profitably spent on the beginning.

First typical symptoms of aging:

1. You can no longer spell! Mrs. Smith the fourth-grade teacher would be scandalised!

2. Your cursive writing looks alien as it slants uphill. It won't bother the millennials because they don't know cursive anyway.

3. You write everything down but lose the list.

4. You consult your calendar frequently during the day. Sometimes you have to consult the sky to see if it's day or night. Most clocks have eliminated the AM/PM designation. Your cell phone will help.

5. You begin to have hesitant speech – finding words is hard and slow.

It is said that aging people have a diminished desire to try new things. They doubt their ability; they expect to be unable to accomplish any new activity. While few start flying lessons or cave diving, based on the number of people over 60 who don the skies to foreign lands each year, that may not be a true saying. Stewards are challenged to find room on planes for the canes, walkers and scooters that bold customers bring with them. Foreign hotels at all levels advertise that they are handicapped accessible.

However, aging experts tout respect for your biological clock by recommending regular hours, better sleep patterns, medication and above all exercising. Gary Small, M.D., director of the UCLA Longevity Center and co-author of The Small Guide to Alzheimer's Disease, says that exercise makes the brain bigger, especially the areas needed for memory. "A bigger brain is a better brain."

Many of us grew up in unhealthy homes with angry or mentally challenged parents. Early lives shape the very hardware of our brains, leaving some people impaired in certain respects, but other people grow up stronger. Maybe your parents should have done some things differently but blaming them is inviting a guilt trip for yourself. Remember, there is no such thing as a perfect parent. How your parents raised you was according to the stresses and resources they had at the time, including their own parental role models. Your parents may be your first role models, but they are not the only factor structuring your personality.

The following chart compares how some survive and flourish and others tend to be duplicating the same toxic environments as their parents:

Negative Affects	Positive Affects
hostile bias	ability to detect threats
recall of negative events	strategic behaviors
self-worth issues	better at task shifting
dysregulated fight-or-flight	cognitive flexibility
acting rashly even unprovoked	fast strategies
feeling disaster pending	creativity
anxiety and depression	tenancy

suspicious nature

self-fulfilling prophecies

missed opportunities

lost in pain and bitterness

victim mentality

blames others

introverted

dreamer

lack of perfectionism

devotion to others

complex character

risk taker

dependability

diligent worker

tolerance for ambiguity

responsive to change

(Author unknown)

There is no recipe for living a bitter negative life no matter what circumstance God placed you in. There is, however, a recipe for living a full positive life and it can be found in Galatians 5:22-23.

EMOTIONS

It is expected that as we age, we become more emotional and develop strong feelings from our circumstances, moods, or relationships. We spend more time analyzing our actions and the emotions that drive them. Emotions can be internal and external responses to events. Why are emotions important to us?

Emotions are feelings and as we interact with others, understanding the emotions that are driving their behavior helps us to respond appropriately. The knowledge of emotions also helps us to understand and perhaps to alter our own feelings as we respond to others.

There is little agreement on the number of emotions that are displayed by the billions of people on this planet, but there are a few basic emotions that almost all fields of study agree on. Most of the Western philosophers propose extensive theories – often competing theories – that try to explain emotion, human action, and its consequences. The primary current theories are listed below:

Number of Emotions:

Discrete Emotion Theory   12

Robert Plutchik's Theory   8

Aristotle's "Rhetoric" Book Two   9

Darwin's theory   34

Univ. of California, Berkeley   27

Paul Ekman's facial expression   6

To understand how emotions help us:

At a seminar, two attendees meet. One looks at the other man and has no recollection of his name or association. The other man runs and catches him in a bear hug. He says, "You old dog, haven't seen you in 10 years, but you look the same".

What does he say and the emotion involved?

"You've got the wrong guy, I don't believe I know you." (emotion: offensive, will make the other guy feel bad/stupid)

"I've been forgetting a lot lately, remind me of when we met." (emotion: kindness, giving him an out, taking responsibility)

"Oh, yeah, I remember you now, how are you? Sorry, I need to hurry." (emotion: self-attention, faking it, and getting rid of him by walking away)

All three feelings – offense, kindness, and self-attention are stimuli for action to the situation. Any of the three emotions could be chosen for this event.

It is easy to read some people by facial expressions or verbal responses. This is because you are familiar with the person and how they usually respond. You would be worried if your best friend responded with a scowl to a suggestion that she had previously originated. It is not so easy to read the expressions of a stranger who might be ill, grieving, or naturally predisposed to negative thinking.

Researchers have found that for all generations, negative emotions decrease with age. In other words,

as people got older, they got less negative. These psychological studies document the tendency of older people to regulate their emotions more effectively than younger people, by maintaining positive feelings and lowering negative feelings. This supports the "socioemotional selectivity" theory that, as people get older and become more aware of the limited time left in life, they direct their attention to more positive thoughts, activities, and memories. The research authors wrote that "With age, people place increasingly more value on emotionally meaningful goals and thus invest more cognitive and behavioral resources in obtaining them." (28)

Physiology may aid the process. The theory of emotional body mapping helps us to understand the connection between emotions and physical feelings and where they live. A 2014 study found that there are 13 emotions and they correspond with certain body parts. Researchers hypothesized that different emotions correspond with different physical reactions. The results showed that, for the participant pool (701 people), different emotions consistently impacted similar areas of the body. Maybe that's where we get our expressions: "cold feet," "a gut reaction," or a shiver down your spine." (29)

Never underestimate the power of emotions in life. By tapping into your emotions, you'll discover what motivates you. Your passions will ignite your vision. Emotions run deep – past your intellect and far into your brain – for what you feel. (30)

One emotion that is easy to describe and evaluate is that of tears. Women have long ago learned the healing power of tears. Men of younger years have viewed tears as unnatural, unmanly, and even a trait exhibited by less virile men. However, as men get older, they seem to be more apt to shed tears when sad, grieving, reminiscing, and feeling extreme joyfulness.

Scientists say that men have lower levels of a hormone found in tears compared with women. Others believe that an emotional response originates in the limbic system which is hard-wired to the nervous system. Regardless of physiological reasons, society judges tearful men, and emotional tears are just one of the mired traits that masculine men must not violate. It may be that men are just better at compartmentalizing. It seems as we age, those walls collapse until feelings are more open and honest.

Most aging persons, men, and women, may shed tears when recalling lost loved ones, lost opportunities, lost loves, wrong decisions, and loss of youthful prowess and beauty. As we age, we seem less concerned about the opinions of others than the assessment of their own lives thus far.

"Tears and weeping seem to be an intractable part of the human condition people weep, even in the Bible – even in England." – David Mitchell

CONVERSATIONS

Randy Travis, the country singer and song-writer, sang about old men talking about the weather and old women talking about old men. He was almost right. Aging adults love to talk, period; to talk about their lives, both good and bad. As we interviewed people who were aging, the five top topics of conversation seemed to focus on physical well-being, weather, sports, grandchildren, and pets.

I physical well-being:

It is amazing that as we age, we tend to drop all of our pretenses of being superhuman and immune to the normal process of aging. When we awaken to the fact that we are getting older – fast, we begin to readily admit to pain, hardship, and frailty. We seek comrades who have like maladies and maybe new information to share.

Other than sleeping problems, the most common physical topics mentioned in our interviews were of arthritis, cancer, TIAs, urination and pain.

Arthritis

"Ole' Arthur's got me this morning…" is a familiar saying among people as they get older.

You are truly blessed if you are one of the few who do not develop arthritis as you age. Arthritis causes swelling, stiffness, and tenderness of the joints and the symptoms gradually increase. Other usual symptoms are redness and range of motion difficulties.

There are many types of arthritis but osteoarthritis and rheumatoid arthritis are the most common types. Osteoarthritis causes cartilage – the hard, slippery tissue that covers the ends of bones where they form a joint – to break down. Rheumatoid arthritis is a disease in which the immune system attacks the joints, beginning with the lining. (37)

You can be susceptible to arthritis if it runs in your family. The incidence is higher if you are a woman, if you are of advanced age, if you have a history of joint injury from sports, or if you are obese. Arthritis is diagnosed by various types of imagery.

Arthritis can be treated, but not cured. NSAIDs relieve pain and reduce inflammation. These meds such as ibuprofen (Advil, Motrin IB, others) and naproxen sodium (Aleve) can cause stomach, heart or stroke problems. Topical creams or gels can sometimes help joint pain. Drastic joint issues may call for surgery: joint repair, replacement or fusion.

Perhaps the most successful treatment for arthritis is what you eat and how much you weigh.

Good foods	Bad foods
Fresh fruits	red meat
leafy greens	high-fat diary
fatty fish	salt, sugar
olive oil	corn
garlic	fried food
turmeric	canned food
walnuts	alcohol
avocados	refined and processed
cinnamon	gluten

If the lists are too complicated, stick to the Mediterranean diet!

Cancer

It is difficult to discuss health challenges without encountering the word cancer. The incidence of that expansive disease impacts us all as victims, caretakers, and survivors.

Most victims of cancer present the condition as hopeless and terrifying. Others tell their stories as natural phenomena of the journey toward death. Due to the mired types, unique impacts, and treatments for cancer, only the most general data is related in this health chapter.

The Centers for Disease Control and Prevention (CDC) reports that cancer is the second leading cause of death in the United States, exceeded only by heart disease. The latest data (2020) states that one of every five deaths in the US is due to cancer: 1 in 9 men and 1 in 12 women.

The International Agency for Research on Cancer (IARC) released a 2022 report, which is a comprehensive overview of the global burden of cancer based on a survey of 115 countries. The report reveals that there were 9.7 million deaths in 2022 (9.96 million were recorded in 2020) and 20 million new cancer cases (19.6 million in 2020). The report cautions that these numbers are estimates for 2022 based on the best available data and do not necessarily show a trend, as previous estimates in 2020 are based on different methodologies resulting from Covid. According to this report, lung cancer and female breast cancer are the most commonly occurring cancers worldwide. Lung cancer (primarily due to smoking) is also the leading cause of cancer deaths worldwide. The rapidly growing global cancer burden reflects both an aging population and growth, as well as changes to people's exposure to risk factors. Tobacco, alcohol, and obesity are key factors behind the increasing incidence of cancer, with air pollution still a key driver of environmental risk factors. (32)

The global incidence of cancer is predicted to increase significantly in the coming decades. Demographic-based predictions indicate that the annual number of new cancer cases will reach 35 million by 2050, representing a 77% increase from the number in 2022.

Despite these frightening statistics, there are approximately 53.5 million people who are alive today more than five years after a diagnosis of cancer. This is probably due to education, early diagnosis, new drug development, advanced surgical techniques, and regular medical follow-ups.

Cancer is no respecter of persons and may run in families: probably due to close members living with the same risks. Efforts to trace the incidence of cancer in an extended family tree are usually not revealing. Death certificates only list the final cause of death which does not always acknowledge the presence of the cancer that has eroded the failed organs. Cancer is mostly a hidden disease, eating away in the body until it destroys a vital organ which results in death.

Like most physical diseases, cancer has been around for eons. In the New Testament, it is described as a "canker" which is an ulcerous condition or disease of a human, or an impact of false teachings. Some translations call it gangrene or a cancerous growth that spreads and causes harm to the body. It is also described as a "rust" as it slowly kills vital organs. Although cancer occurs in people of all ages (even children) it is likely that in the aged it occurs most frequently: given more time for the "rust" to ravage and destroy.

2 Timothy 2:17 and James 3:5

are related to "canker."

Urination

All of us, every day, get direct and important health feedback from our bladder. Research indicates that the bladder has a direct line of communication with the brain to tell us when the bladder is full.

A lot of our conversations surround the intricacies of urination (peeing). Our peeing habits change as we get older. Around the age of 50, our kidneys stop filtering fluid as well as they once did – causing concentrated urine, irritating the bladder and causing critical urges. Sharing information with our friends about these changes without embarrassment is a trait shared by most aging persons.

Jokes are freely told about pee. When you get a bladder infection, urine trouble is a popular one. Never since elementary school, when third-grade boys sprayed the bathroom walls to see who could pee the farthest, have men shared the subject so freely. Frequency, reluctance, and incontinence are discussed openly and often.

Women are subject to the same issues, but they usually have a grander audience than men. Did you ever wonder why women go to the bathroom in pairs or groups? They couldn't all have the urge to pee at the same time. It is to talk (gossip?) but instead of "tea time," it becomes "pee time" for them. Whatever the reason, bless them.

When young, peeing was quick, easy, and thoughtless. Urination could be held for a day if other activities prohibited it. Now, attention to sudden urges and bathroom locations dominates our strategic planning when in unfamiliar places and outings.

Despite the jokes and ease of conversation, we must remember that the unitary system is responsible for maintaining the volume of bodily fluids within normal limits as it excretes the waste of the body. If the unitary system fails, there are no other organs that can take over and compensate adequately.

Frequent urination is the need to pee more often than average (seven to eight times) throughout the day. It can happen to anyone, but it's more common in people over the age of 70, pregnant people, and people with an enlarged prostate. The most common cause is urinary tract infection.

It's common to occasionally wake up at night to pee. In general, you can expect to pee once a night in your 40s and 50s, twice a night in your 60s and 70s, and even two to three times a night in your 80s and beyond. Waking up too often in the night can keep you from getting enough sleep and is sometimes a sign of a health condition. (33)

If you don't pee enough, it can also lead to a variety of health problems. A healthy bladder can hold about 2 cups of urine before it's considered full. It takes your body 9 to 10 hours to produce 2 cups of urine. That's about as long as you can wait without the possibility of damaging your organs. If you hold your pee as a matter of habit, your bladder can start to atrophy. Over time, you may develop incontinence. (34)

Contributing to the problem is that we don't get thirsty like we used to which determines how much we void. Seven or eight glasses of liquid a day is not typically a reality for aging persons. Remember, no input – less output.

Peeing problems can often be a symptom of other serious illnesses. Men are susceptible to enlarged prostates which hinder urination. Women are acutely susceptible to bladder infections.

Dr. Ava Oates, a psychologist specializing in the care of the elderly residing in facilities, states that if a patient has a bladder infection, they also have thinking, relating, and slow brain problems which negates any mental therapy. Dr. Oates also has found that bladder infections are easily tied to mental stresses even in restrictive residences.

An old marine loved to tell about one of his buddies who voided and then sat in the "head" every morning while eating an apple!

TIAs

As we age, there is nothing that terrifies us more than losing control of our lives through a stroke which makes us totally dependent on others. Many of the people we interviewed described the experience of having a transient ischemic attack (a mini-stroke). A transient ischemic attack is a short period of symptoms similar to those of a stroke. It's caused by a brief blockage of blood flow to the brain.

A TIA usually lasts only a few minutes or hours and leaves no long-term damage. However, a TIA is considered a warning or precursor for a more devastating full-fledged stroke. The TIA can be repeated for days or even within a year unless the source of the blockage is found and eliminated.

Usual symptoms of a TIA are: confusion, slurred speech, inadequate perception, skewed vision, numbness or weakness in the extremities (usually on one side of the body), dizziness, balance and coordination problems, and a pronounced fear of imminent death. Of course, every repeat TIA may be different because of the mired areas of the brain that might be affected.

There is a tendency among TIA victims to downplay the initial event. They use such excuses as new or forgotten medicine, lack of sleep, eating habits, excessive worry, etc. to deny the seriousness of this short-term loss of control. However, the possibility of a recurrence lingers. Repeated TIAs heighten the expectation that the body is sending a clear message. Your trusted PCP is the best source of information and referral.

We have heard of close relatives who had "spells" and eventually succumbed to a major stroke. There are risks of a TIA or a stroke depending on family history, age (especially after age 55), sex (men at higher risk), prior attack, and co-mingling diseases such as diabetes, sickle cell, and COVID-19.

Lifestyle choices also play a major role in the risks of TIAs and strokes. Smoking, inactivity, high blood pressure, poor nutrition, drinking, using controlled drugs, and maintaining a healthy weight are all changes within our grasp to lessen the occurrence of mini- and/or major strokes.

"I feel that I have this disaster hanging over my head. It scares me that a stroke may hit me at any time. I may not be able to prevent it no matter what I do."

" … God did not give us a spirit of timidity, but a spirit of power, of love and of self-discipline". 2 Timothy 1:7.

Pain

The Lord gave us a magnificent and complex body, perfectly engineered for efficient maintenance and sustainability. He also gave us pain as a warning that something was interfering with that efficiency.

The body has 11 systems with integral parts, which are assigned specific tasks to keep us healthy:

skeletal	digestive

muscular	urinary

cardiovascular	endocrine

respiratory	lymphatic

nervous	reproductive	integumentary

The interruptions to the functioning of a sound body can be found both in scripture and in history. Biblical examples include Jacob's limp, Paul's thorn in the flesh, and of course Job and his host of disorders. While Job was eventually restored whole, Jacob and Paul may have lived with pain for a lifetime (however, it didn't stop their progress in finding and achieving God's purpose for each of them.)

Pain has a physical purpose: as an alarm to protect us so we can live longer and to teach us the limits of stress that our body can endure before bodily damage. It also has a spiritual purpose: to test our faith, to wean us from the world, to call us to heavenly hope, to reveal to us what we really love, to teach us obedience, to reveal God's compassion, to strengthen us for greater usefulness and to enable us to comfort others in their trials. (35)

We experience pain differently; some have a high pain tolerance and some have a low tolerance. My friend Betty, was diagnosed with stage four cancer, she experienced no pain, and survived her treatment without a complaint. Another friend, Kathy, becomes tearful over a paper cut. Both women are

Christians who believe in the will of God. They just feel pain differently.

Various factors contribute to this phenomenon:

<u>genetic predispositions</u> – certain genes may impact the production of endorphins, the body's natural pain relievers.

<u>psychological influences</u> – such as resilience, coping mechanisms, and previous experiences with pain.

<u>sensory perception variability</u> – factors such as nerve sensitivity, pain receptors, and central nervous system processing influence how individuals interpret and respond to pain. (36)

Researchers and healthcare providers can develop tailored pain management strategies that account for the unique needs and experiences of each individual. Medications sometimes help with pain. Of course, medications do not repair the site of the pain but they can temporarily deal with the pain messages to the brain.

The are a few individuals who feel no pain at all. Brain damage, whether congenital or a result of injury, can destroy the brain and pain receptors. While this might seem ideal, it also leaves the individual in continuous danger. Imagine a cut that you do not know about until the blood starts dripping or the burn from accidentally brushing against a stove or open flame. Adults with no sense of pain tend to have significant orthopedic injuries that won't heal properly because a lack of pain stops people from restricting activities. (37)

We can be thankful for the doctors and research-ers who spend their lives seeking ways to help us with pain. My granddaughter has spent 17 years training before starting to practice as a fertility spe-cialist. But she, and probably most doctors, would be the first to say that despite their efforts, it is God who decides whether the patient recovers or not.

2 Chronicles 16:13 relates the story of King Asa and reminds us that while doctors can assist, it is essential to seek God's guidance and healing in times of illness.

"Is there no balm in Gilead; is there no physician there? Why then is not the health of the daughter of my people recovered?" Jeramiah 8:22.

#2. Pets:

"My dog can tell when I am depressed. My cat tells me when she is depressed." "What if my dog returns the ball because he thinks I'm having fun?"

Another favorite topic of conversation for senior adults is that of pets. Most people who live alone have a dog for company and/or protection. The exploits of that beloved animal give much fodder for sharing how faithful, how intelligent, how brave, and how dependable.

According to the AARP The Magazine of April/May, 2019, forty percent of people in their 70s own a pet. Older adults who walk their dogs have a healthier body weight, go to the doctor less often, get more exercise, and mix and mingle with other people more frequently than those without dogs. The American Heart Association says "Dogs are heart-healthy messengers." Even a cuddly, toy-size dog provides 15 percent lower risk of early death according to a Swedish study of 3.4 million adults.

We tend to humanize the traits of canine pets and brag about how much they understand and perform. Have you ever heard of anyone bragging about their cat? Some people talk to their dogs (baby talk?). Others dress their dogs in clothes for holidays and special occasions and present them with Christmas and birthday presents. Some sleep with their pet(s). Many report taking their dog to "doggie daycare" to prevent loneliness while the master is absent. This gives a whole new meaning to the "dog's day" of the past.

Presently there are a lot of pet owners who have their animals certified as emotional support, avoiding many restrictive laws. The March 2024 AARP Bulletin quotes the American Kennel Club estimation of tens of thousands of service dogs assisting a wide range of human needs in our nation.

Dogs are expensive. Designer dogs cost upwards of $2,500. when they are born. Food is around $100.00 per month, grooming is $75.00 every six weeks, low-cost insurance is $30.00 per month and vet bills are equal to people's doctors. An interesting exercise is to complete a two-column chart labeled costs and the other benefits. In the left-hand column put all the expenses of keeping the dog (pet) and in the right-hand column list all the benefits of having the dog (pet).

When most people try to do this exercise, they become frustrated and sometimes angry - "It feels like I am trying to justify keeping one of my kids" Exactly! Pets are family members, entitled to the same love and respect as any other member of the family.

Dogs have shorter lives than we do, the larger the dog, the shorter the life. So dog lovers may have lost several dogs throughout life. As each pet expires, the grief is palpable. That grief spurs the question: do all dogs go to heaven?

This question has been asked by animal lovers for centuries, and even some noted theologians have weighed in on the issue. According to many of them, animals probably do go to heaven.

C. S. Lewis, a well-known apologist for the Christian faith in the 1900s, Rev. Billy Graham, America's pastor, and Martin Luther, the well known reform leader of the 16th century and the founder of the Lutheran Church, all conclude that animals do to to Heaven based on God's subtle but clear word that all creation (except for demons and unbelievers) are lining up for His love.

So, do dogs, cats, horses, and other pets go to heaven? While the Bible doesn't come straight out and say "yes" it does imply through its discussion of the redemption of God's creation that our pets will greet us in the new heaven and new earth. (38)

When discussing this issue with a 77-year-old pet lover: "You've lost so many pets over the years – if they are all waiting for you in heaven, how are you going to take care of the menagerie there?" She answered "My Mom and Dad will be waiting there for me too. They will help me care for my pets as they did on earth." What faith!

And no matter the final circumstances between pet and owner, the dogs, like children, are the most forgiving beings that God created on earth and will recreate in heaven (cats carry grudges!).

#3 Grandchildren

Blessed is the gift of grandchildren, a lasting link to our worldly existence.

We claim bragging rights on grandchildren over that of our own children.

The way our children turned out was the result of our many parenting mistakes. The way our grandchildren turn out is the result of the parenting by our imperfect child plus unknown traits from an unrelated person.

Speaking of bragging, friends can be annoyed by excessive conversation about your grandchildren. Of course, you recognize that the grandchildren of others are not as beautiful/handsome, intelligent, talented or successful as yours. But be sensitive and provide equal bragging time!

You are blessed if you have many grandchildren. In the United States, people are starting families later and have fewer children. With access to more reliable contraception, goals of education, and careers, they are delaying becoming parents before taking on the all-consuming responsibilities of child-rearing. This tendency results in our becoming grandparents at 50, 60, or even 70 years old which makes us unable to respond to the active needs or requests of little ones.

To be fair, some couples desperately want to have children but cannot because of physical reasons and cannot afford the assisted reproductive technologies such as in vitro fertilization.

Researchers tell us that ovaries age at a markedly accelerated rate compared with other organs in the body. Also, the sperm quality of men declines significantly over 40 and continues to decline thereafter. All of this information would encourage us to recommend to our children to have their children, if possible, before the age of 40.

At any age, our grandchildren accept us for ourselves, without rebuke or effort to change us. No one in our entire lives has ever done this, not our parents, siblings, spouses, friends – and hardly ever our grown children. (39)

An aggravation mentioned by many grandparents is that every conversation, visit, schedule or gift between the child and grandparent has to be filtered through the parent (usually the mother). This sends a clear message that the grandparent does not occupy a permanent chair in the private family group.

An old joke is that grandchildren are precious because they can be given back to the parents. That is not true of the 2.5 million US grandparents who are having to step up and raise children of their children. This situation can be due to poverty, substance abuse, death, extended military deployment, or simply the lack of caring. At a time when aging parents are healthier, wealthier, and have greater expectations, they are called upon to care for a second generation of children.

We are called upon to learn a new vocabulary in dealing with our grandchildren. What do you call a cohabitating couple, (even with children) boyfriend, girlfriend, or fiancé? The old term "common law" marriage has expired, possibly because it carries a lengthier association. How do you respond to a wedding invitation for a couple that has been living together for years and possesses all the material goods imaginable? How do you ask friends about their adult grandchildren who live in different (and sinful) arrangements?

It has been said that if you question how your grandchildren will remember you when you're gone, think of how you remember your grandparents compared to your own growing up years. There will not be much difference. But play a mind video of how you remember your children growing up compared to your grandchildren and there may be a lot of differences.

Do we live in a brave new world or a fearful new world, you decide!

#4 Weather:

Everyone is an expert in predicting the weather. Professional weather forecasting is the prediction of the weather through the application of the principles of physics, supplemented by a variety of statistical and empirical techniques. In addition to predictions of atmospheric phenomena themselves, weather forecasting includes predictions of changes on earth's surface caused by atmospheric conditions—e.g., snow and ice cover, storm tides, and floods. Forecasters use multiple methods for predicting the weather including climatology, analog, persistence and trends, and the mathematical method. (40)

You can expect to encounter a lot of weather experts – not on TV, radio, or computers, but around the lunch table. Most predictions are based on history. "It snowed here in 2017 and 2021, therefore, it will snow again this year." (climatology) "On Friday, October 10, 2012, the weather was exactly like today." (analog) "Today, it appears that the weather will be calm." (persistence and trends method) "The computer forecasts…" (mathematical)

It is said that forecasters can only predict the weather on average 50% of the time. However, according to the National Oceanic and Atmospheric Administration (NOAA), a seven-day forecast can accurately predict the weather about 80 percent of the time, and a five-day forecast can accurately predict the weather in approximately 90 percent of the time. Predicting the weather is more difficult in the United States due to the vastness of the country compared to many smaller countries.

Weather forecasts are not perfect and can be affected by many factors. The further into the future the forecast goes, the less reliable the estimate.

If you can't trust professional forecasters, try Grandpa's arthritic knee!

#5. Sports

Sportscasters are the true 50% predictors. Someone must win and someone must lose. The wins build momentum, and the losses build character. When the journey ends in victory, it will always seem like a victory march which makes perfect sense when considered in retrospect. (41) Sports fans can recall all the correct things that their team did and how it led to the victory. They can also reiterate all the bad actions that resulted in the other team losing.

Sportscasters and players are predominantly male, despite the enactment of Title IX. That landmark law ensured gender equality in educational opportunities. When that law passed, only 7% of high school athletes were girls. Today it's 42%. However, both interest and participation in organized sports is still a predominantly male thing.

Time magazine reported a 2013 study that found males were twice as likely as females to be involved or interested in sports across 50 different countries or cultures

The most popular spectator sport worldwide is soccer which is played by both women and men. Although women's soccer is growing in popularity, the majority of fans following female games are men. While gender distinctions are not absolute, cultural norms and historical biases have always influenced sports participation and popularity.

Men's love for sports is a complex interplay of physiology, culture, and social dynamics. Men seek to prove their prowess vicariously through playing and watching sports competitions. At the end of the game, there is always an analysis of each player's precision, the strategy of the coach, and the fairness of the officials. The game is rehashed and dissected until the next competition.

Women also love sports but play for different reasons. Women usually do not care who wins team games unless they are players, and when the game is over, it is a closed subject. Individual sports are more popular with women athletes where the focus is on one's own performance, not outdoing others. In our interviews with women, the subject of sports was rarely mentioned, unless expressed in conjunction with the activities of husband, sons, etc.

<u>Sports Fans</u>

There are fans of sports that identify with the team no matter if they win or lose. Although dejected by a loss, these rabid fans continue to sport tee shirts, hats, and signs to express their loyalty to the team and predict a "wait until the next time" attitude: not for revenge, but for justice. They know about the statistics and history of each player and religiously follow the progress of the team, no matter the emotional or financial cost.

In recent articles, psychologists believe that sports teams and their followers satisfy the following needs of the fans:

- losses help prepare us for the worst of life
- we feel better about ourselves when our team wins
- identification with a team unifies us

- allows socially acceptable exhibitionism

- serves as a laboratory for superstition

- serves as a safe outlet for love/hate emotions

- provides vicarious fun for all ages

Sports continue to captivate and unite us all. It must have been so forever; St. Paul uses the analogy of his life as a good fight, and the finish of a race. (2 Timothy 4:7).

FORGIVENESS

One of the struggles of aging is regret – regret for actions you have taken and regret for what others have done to you over the years, especially when you were a child:

1. Being given inappropriate or burdensome responsibilities

2. Not being fed or provided a safe place to live

3. Being hit or smacked by your parents/ grandparents

4. Having an emotionally unavailable parent who withholds affection

5. Being "punished", kicking, shaking, biting, burning, hair pulling, etc.

6. Being a child of divorce

7. Being called names or verbally insulted

8. Abandonment - left for long periods without a babysitter

9. Emotional neglect - not being nurtured, or encouraged

10. Critizing your personality or appearance.

11. Destruction of personal belongings

12. Humiliation

13. Molestation

14. Accidents: car, fire, or other spontaneous traumatic events.

There are many other traumatic events, depending on the circumstances.

Peggy Y. Boone, Ph.D.

An elderly man shared this story:

"I was barely 12 years old and was babysitting with my four nieces and nephews while my sister worked. My sister and her husband were going through a nasty divorce and were fighting over who would get the kids.

They were good kids and listened to me as I fixed lunch and played with them. Just as we finished lunch, their father drove up. Of course, the kids jumped up and ran to him; they hadn't seen him for quite a while. He told them to get their clothes and get in his car. They didn't hesitate, although the youngest little boy said,

"Does my Mama know?" The bigger kids shoved him into the car.

I tried to intervene by telling Sam that my sister would be mad at me if he took the kids and that she gave me the responsibility for them. I even tried to prevent the youngest boy from getting into the car. Sam was a very strong man, and easily shoved me aside and took off with the kids. They were happy as they left, and we soon heard that Sam and the kids became residents of another state.

The first words from my sister were, 'Why did you let him take them?' She was angry at me for a long time. She did eventually forgive me but she never regained custody of the kids. I don't know who to be mad at: my sister for leaving a twelve-year-old to watch four kids, my uncle Sam who took the kids, the kids who were so eager to leave, or myself for not doing more. Although it has been 50 years, I have never forgiven myself.

Lewis Smedes, the renowned Christian author, ethicist and theologian, says there are three levels of forgiveness. First, we rediscover the humanity of the person who hurt us. That simply means that without diminishing their sin, we admit that they are a sinner just like we are sinners. Second, we surrender our right to get even. It is natural to want someone else to pay for all the pain they caused us. But in the end, we must leave all judgment in the hands of a just and merciful God. Third, we revise our feelings toward the other person. This means giving up our hatred and letting go of our bitterness. Ultimately, it means taking Jesus seriously when he said, "Love your enemies, bless those who curse you, do good to those who hate you, and pray for those who spitefully use you and persecute you." (Matthew 5:44). You'll know you have reached total forgiveness when you can ask God to bless those who have hurt you so deeply. This is indeed a high standard, so high that without God it is impossible. That's why Smedes calls forgiveness a miracle. He's right. Total forgiveness is nothing less than a miracle of God. (42)

Other authors remind us that forgiveness starts with a decision to let go of the resentment:

> It is not letting the offender off the hook.

It does not mean forgetting.

It does not revert us to repeatedly being a victim.

It is a process, not an event.

It is not based on others' actions but on our attitude.

It is not a topic of conversation with others.

It does not always have to be reported to the other person.

It does not require you to reconcile with the person who harmed you.

If withheld, it is a refusal to let go of perceived power.

It is returning to God the right to take care of justice.

Forgiveness is a powerful tool that can bring peace of mind and free the forgiver from corrosive anger. Experts agree that it involves letting go of deeply held negative feelings. It empowers you to recognize the pain you suffered without letting that pain define you, enabling you to heal and move on with your life. (43)

Forgiveness doesn't excuse the behavior of others. Forgiveness prevents their behavior from destroying our hearts. It is up to us if we are a prisoner of our past or a guardian of our future. It is our bridge to cross.

"...if you do not forgive others their trespasses, neither will your Father forgive your trespasses." Matthew 6:15.

MEMORIES

"**You** never know the value of a moment until it becomes a memory." – Dr. Seuss

As our brains sift and classify information, some is discarded and some is retained for use in the future in the form of memories.

Memory is the power or process of reproducing or recalling what has been learned and retained, especially through associative mechanisms. (Merriam-Webster Dictionary)

Mary Pipher in Women Rowing North, says that most discussions about memory in old people concern deterioration and loss, but such discussions miss an the important phenomenon, our minds become less cluttered and more concerned with essentials. (44) Therefore, the memories that we have no occasion to use are, in effect, dormant.

Although modern scientists are engaged in finding a way to totally erase memories that are unwanted, it is generally thought that every experience good or bad is retained in the brain. Some of those memories never resurface, but others are strengthened by frequent use. Every time we recall an event or conversation, it grows easier to remember and often without a "trigger."

Triggers are memories that surface when we encounter events or objects similar to something (event, conversation, emotion), that we have experienced before.

A simple example:

As a pre-teenager, when visiting a favorite aunt, she called attention to a pimple on my face in front of my cousins who at the time had perfect skin.

Even as an adult, every time I see a small blemish on my face, I recall the humiliation I felt. I think of that episode and the verbal carelessness of my aunt. Then the present blemish seems larger and more important.

It is easier to refresh this memory the next time I see a blemish.

As we age, we begin to complain about not remembering people, places, and things. We enter rooms and cannot remember why we came there.

We spend a lot of time looking for things. We use notes, lists, and calendars to remind us of activities. We forget the names of people who we haven't seen for a while. We even sometimes have to call the role of our children to talk to the correct one.

We also tend to tell the same stories over and over to the same audience. We have new and creative ideas, but cannot express them fully. All that is normal.

What is not normal is the loss of memories of how to negotiate in the world. We've got things to do, people to see, bills to pay. It will be, as we age, more and more difficult to do these things efficiently. We even begin to find driving a task and a symbolic thing. Giving up that privilege voluntarily or forcibly is giving up hope of ever being self-sufficient again.

Memories begin with our five senses through our experiences of the world. When one or more of these senses fail, memories can be lost. None of this should be especially surprising when you consider the layered richness of memory – the distant sights, sounds, smells, feelings, and conversations that can be evoked by something as ephemeral as a scent on the breeze. (45)

In the past, it was believed that there was a special "compartment" or location within the brain that stores memories. Now it is known that memories are distributed throughout the structure of the brain. That is why the treatment for Alzheimer's is so elusive. Memories can be lost in just one of the structures: brain stem, motor, language, auditory, and emotional centers, and it can impair the tenets of livelihood.

In the AARP Bulletin of June 2018, research is reported that what older people believe recalling in the aftermath of a conversation or encounter may actually be a false memory. As people age, the brain resources devoted to recalling details diminish. We remember the event, but not the specifics. The brain can trick us by filling in the details with false images so that they make sense and feel real. To manage false recall, it is suggested that we write down critical information, focusing on a couple of important details instead of the entire scene.

Once upon a time never comes again and the recollection of an event may not be entirely accurate given a time-lapse and our own interpretation or wishes. Perhaps that is why in scripture we are told to have up to three witnesses to testify to a crime. (Deuteronomy 19:16) and why modern law enforcement agencies do not rely on the testimony of a single witness.

In the early aging years, we tend to vividly recall negative memories that are tied to pain, hurt, or revenge in some way. As we get older, we learn that revenge is not our job. We begin to use selective memory and leave the bad or unpleasant memories forgotten.

Forgetting memories is one way to erase those unpleasant memories. Forgetting serves as the filter that diminishes the stuff that the brain deems unimportant. We do this by not calling up the memory that is no longer useful. Then our negative memories grow dim and the pleasant ones are recalled more often so as not to forget how important and useful they are to us.

"Forget the former things; do not dwell on the past."
Isaiah 43:18.

SECRETS

One of the most popular slogans of Alcoholics Anonymous is "You're only as sick as your secrets." Initially, new members are encouraged to share their secrets in small supportive groups. Later, some members move out to larger more diverse groups to acknowledge and heal addictions and related issues. A major component of the program is the enlistment of a sponsor. This sponsor is regularly available to the alcoholic to listen, advise, support, and intervene if needed. This sharing of secrets has been effectively restoring the lives of alcoholics for 85 years.

We all keep secrets. Secrets are a universal human phenomenon; everyone has something to hide and it starts early. It can begin in childhood as we struggle to connect our behaviors with the rules of our parents without thinking of the possible subsequent punishment.

An example is the 5-year-old who used his father's phone and credit card to order a toy from Amazon, addressed to himself. He was smart enough to do the deed without a thought to the cover-up necessary to escape the consequences when the package arrived.

We can remember that kids use keeping secrets as a way to bond with others.

To tell a secret to a friend is a badge of trust and to hear a secret is an honor.

Although youngsters cannot remember what their parents or teachers say, they will hold the shared secret zealously.

As we age, our secrets become more involved, and we share them more carefully. Most researchers in the field list these topics among normal secret examples:

1. Hurting another person

2. Abuse of drugs

3. Sexual behavior

4. Romantic desire

5. Theft

6. Lie

7. Violation of trust

8. Physical self-harm

9. Abortion

10. Financial secret

Among 50,000 research participants, the most common secrets include a lie we've told (69%), romantic desire (61%), sex (58%), and finances (58%). (46)

Secrets can be a burden to the secret carrier. Secrets can be light or heavy but both are impossible not to regularly visit in the mind. The more our minds ruminate on something as high stakes as a secret, the worse we feel. The thoughts of the secret can crowd out happier thoughts that we deserve to enjoy.

Most of the literature records that the burdens of secrets can do physical and mental harm to secret holders and recommends the sharing of the secret for relief. However, the trusted friend, cohort, etc. will then have the burden of guarding the secret. There also must be a promise not ever to violate the trust, which is an awesome responsibility. The next time you hear "Can you keep a secret?" maybe you should reply "I'm not very good at that."

As we age, most of us desire to clear out our possessions, memories, and secrets. As all this is shared, children are sometimes shocked that Dad was not Mom's first love, there was an earlier marriage, that there are other families or siblings, or that the happiest time of life was before they were born. Young children assume that their parents (especially their mom) only started to live when the child was born. That assumption lingers until the child has his own child.

Sara Eckel in the November/December 2019 Psychology Today echoes phycologist Carl Pickhardt's belief that parents should not keep secrets from their children. Parents are a well of personal experiences if they will allow their adolescents to know them. Offering older children a more complete and nuanced portrait of a parent can aid their development into adulthood. Such an exchange can help parents cultivate an adult relationship with their child in which all participants' boundaries are honored.

Before sharing long-kept secrets at the end of life, It would be well to consider:

1. What will my secret help?

2. Who might it hurt?

3. Will it damage my reputation/memory?

4. What questions will it raise?

If the need to tell the secret is to seek a clean slate for meeting God, He already knows!

DEPRESSION

Depression is a serious mood disorder. It can affect the way you feel, act, and think. Depression is a common problem among older adults, but clinical depression is not a normal part of aging. Studies show that most older adults feel satisfied with their lives, despite having more illnesses or physical problems than younger people. (47)

Depression is the body's way of blocking the mind's pain. It numbs physical and emotional functions. It generally results when a person internalizes anger or feels a deep sense of loss or powerlessness. Depressed people begin to lack energy and gradually withdraw even from family members. They become emotionally numb or unfeeling toward any responsibility for the needs of others. Depression can also cause chronic physical pain and illness. Victims truly believe they have no hope for restoration.

Depressed people have distorted thinking which is all-or-nothing thinking. They look at things in absolute, black-and-white categories. They view a negative event as a never-ending pattern of defeat. They dwell on the negatives in their lives and ignore the positives. (48)

Since the COVID-19 pandemic, there has been a marked increase in the prevalence of depression. This may be a result of the inactivity of the period, the restrictive environments, the lack of social contact, and the perceived loss of economic progress.

Because the term "depressed" is so common in our society, it can be overused for evasiveness, lack of responsibility, laziness, and feelings of enti-tlement. We therefore must understand some basic facts about the mood disorder:

1. depressive manifestations are differ-ent depending on the person. Not every-one who is depressed openly expresses the pain. Neither does depression excuse bad behavior.

2. thinking positively cannot change depres-sion. It may lead to more depression due to the falseness of the effort.

3. the impact of depression is difficult to under-stand and/or diagnose.

4. depression can be successfully treated but can't be "cured." Psychotherapy and medi-cations may help the depressed to live a more normal life, but the hidden symptoms are

still there. Symptoms may resurface when severe stress, loss, failure or disappointment appears.

5. Severe depression can lead to thoughts of despair, loneliness, and sometimes suicidal tendencies.

Because depression is a serious mood disorder we must be aware of some common symptoms:

- sadness
- hopelessness
- Irritability/anxiety
- loss of interest
- fatigue
- difficulty concentrating
- difficulty sleeping
- weight change
- thoughts of death or suicide

As we get older, body changes can affect the way medicines are absorbed and used. Because of these changes, there can be a larger risk of drug interactions as you age. Share information about all medications and supplements you're taking with your doctor or pharmacist. Health approaches, like yoga, are tried by some to improve well-being and cope with stress which can cause depression. However, there is little evidence to suggest that these approaches, on their own, can successfully treat depression. They should not replace medical treatment.

Personal complementary treatments for depression include physical activity, 7-9 hours of sleep each night, social groups, conversations, journaling, and group hobbies. Other than seeking contact with old friends, social media is not suggested. The exaggerated activities of the posts may trigger feelings of isolation and possible economic disadvantage in the depressed individual.

~ 152 ~

"The Lord himself goes before you and will be with you; he will never leave you nor forsake you. Do not be afraid; do not be discouraged." Deuteronomy 31:8

SHAME

"Aren't you ashamed" has been a long-time common dialogue of a parent trying to shape good behavior in a young child. The child may be puzzled and become angry when a parent attacks the worth of the child rather than the issue: "You always spill your milk… you spilled it this morning… I've told you time and again to be careful… how can you be so clumsy?" Granted, one such interchange will not have consequences in adulthood, but such regular events may produce lifetime feelings of guilt, shame, and even perpetual anger.

There is a difference between guilt and shame. Guilt is a failure to meet the standards of others. In the above scenario, this was Mother's standard. Shame is a failure to meet your own standard of behavior. The child's standard was to please Mother. He didn't meet his standard or that of his mother, so he was bad. With this foundation, adults too can suffer transgressions that trigger the emotions of guilt and shame.

Shame then is closely related to, but distinct from guilt. While shame is a failure to meet your own standards of behavior, guilt is a failure to meet others' standards of behavior. Shame tells us "You have not done your best" and guilt tells us "You have harmed another... you have ignored the golden rule." Shame is personal, while guilt is public. Shame is "I am bad" while guilt is "I did something bad". Shame reflects on the "human being", and guilt reflects on the "human doing". Shame results in internal sanctions – I feel bad – while guilt results in external sanctions – I will be punished. (49)

When interviewed about guilt and shame, the aging adults readily acknowledged many guilty actions they regretted but were more reluctant to share their shameful actions. For those who did admit to actions that shamed them, the tendency was to blame others leading to the episodes. This is a dangerous viewpoint and keeps one from admitting responsibility for the humiliation of actions. It also prevents us from taking actions that are necessary for recovery from shameful behavior.

Those recovery actions may include the following:

1. Talk to a professional about your shame; do not ruminate on it.

2. Examine what you did and what you should have done.

3. Write down the results of the examination.

4. If others were involved and hurt, make amends with them if possible.

5. Concentrate on what you can change and let go of what you cannot.

6. Create steps to reestablish your sense of pride in making good decisions.

"Shame is the most powerful master emotion. It's the fear that we're not good enough." – Brene Brown

"No pit is so deep that He is not deeper still." - Corrie Ten Boom

"When pride comes, then comes shame. But with humility is wisdom." Prov. 11:2.

RESPECT

"When I was a boy of 14, my father was so ignorant I could hardly stand to have the old man around. But when I got to be 21, I was astonished how much the old man had learned in seven years." – Mark Twain

"We know a lot because we've seen a lot." - TV ad for Farmer's Insurance

"My Dad, who never attended school, was the smartest man I ever knew." – Evelyn Dodson

Despite all the advances made for aging persons during the past decades:, such as health, wealth, fitness, independence, etc., the one trait that eludes us is the current respect for our wisdom.

Wisdom is the appropriate application of knowledge. There was a time when age was a pre-requisite for wisdom. Advanced years were revered, and a little gray hair was a small price to pay for all the accumulated wisdom ready to be shared. Now it seems that it is increasingly a loved generation but not considered a very learned one as technology and the subsequent manipulation of the human environ-ment pass us by. We would argue that younger peo-ple have the knowledge over us, but the appropriate application into wisdom eludes most of them.

Portia Nelson, the noted singer, songwriter, actress, and author, shared this concept in her "hole in the sidewalk" poem:

An Autobiography in Five Short Paragraphs

1.

I walk down the street. There is a deep hole in the sidewalk. I fall in. I am lost. I am helpless. It isn't my fault. It takes forever to find a way out.

2.

I walk down the street. There is a deep hole in the sidewalk. I pretend I don't see it. I fall in. I can't believe I'm in the same place, but it isn't my fault. It will take a long time to get out.

3.

I walk down the street. There is a deep hole in the sidewalk. I see it is there. I still fall in. It's a habit. My eyes are open. I know where I am. It is my fault. I get out immediately.

4.

I walk down the street. There is a deep hole in the sidewalk. I walk around it.

5.

I walk down a different street. (50)

Knowledge + experience + opportunity = Wisdom

Perhaps the multi-generational family of the previous generations fostered the view that the oldest person in the family had to be the wisest. Then, when social security, Medicare, Medicaid, and other programs made the aged more independent, families were separated into units. Younger heads then prevailed and, in part, made poor decisions. The counsel of the aged is either not sought or is generally ignored. As our brains work to reshuffle and discard unused information, untapped wisdom may become lost forever.

Fortunately, there is now a higher percentage of people living in homes where there are at least two generations of adults, than since 1950. Currently,

20% of the US population lives with multiple generations under one roof. Much of the increase is attributed to the growing number of Hispanic and Asian families, which are more likely to be multi-generational.

Research shows that living with other generations has physical and mental health benefits. People living in two-generation households have lower premature mortality than those on their own. The generations learn from each other as long there is mutual respect.

"Honesty is the first chapter of the book of wisdom."

"Recently, my dear grandson informed me that I couldn't possibly learn how to use a smartphone like the one permanently attached to his hand. Guess how I earned my post-graduate degree was not learning!"

It is a usual thing to poke fun at the hazards of growing older. Go into any bookstore and ask the location of books on aging and they are all found in the section on humor. Comedians find much fodder to use in ridiculing the disabilities of age such as hearing, sight, and mobility.

"There is a bonus for growing older. Young men and women are eager to help you in the grocery store, ready to help you unload the car, open doors, etc. Your children are anxious to drive you to doctor visits and do other errands. Surely there is much love surrounding you."

Perhaps the loss of the honor of wisdom is the fault of the aging themselves. Older folks also love to tell jokes about old people, perhaps to excuse their own inclinations and actions. People wear tee shirts (probably presented by their children) proclaiming age-related slogans:

> It's weird being the same age as old people, I don't know how to act my age, I've never been this old before, Youth and enthusiasm are no match for old age and treachery, I'm not old, I'm a classic, My body knows how old I am but my mind refuses to believe it, Grandpa knows everything if he doesn't know he makes stuff up really fast.

Do you hear many jokes about 25, 35, 45-year-olds? Maybe aging adults should be brave enough to confront the young with the admonishment that if blessed, they too will be old someday very soon. They know it, but don't believe it!

Suppose that a young person happens to seek wisdom from his grandfather. It would behoove the grandfather not to use experience or his history to formulate an answer. That time was different, the facts are not the same. Instead, the answer should focus on what is relative today, what the young person knows about. An example question might be: "How do you think we can solve the illegal immigrant crisis facing the nation today?" The grandfather might say: "Well, it's different now, we cannot absorb all of the people of the world who might need asylum. However, we might try to elect candidates who have compassion for their plight. We could enact swift new immigration rules that would allow larger quotas and hire more people to process papers faster to help people come to our country legally."

With that answer, the grandson may walk away with things to think about, and one of them might be that grandfather could be more on the ball than he had ever thought. Or, the kid might think that he knew all of that already, and the grandfather had wasted his time.

The most telling story about how some young people view the aged was within the recent presentation by a local paramedic first responder. He described a patient as TDOTL (too damn old to live). One wonders about the level of assistance that the patient received!

"Rise in the presence of the aged, show respect for the elderly and revere your God..." Leviticus 19:32.

TIME

We can expect the occasional feeling that we are running out of time. But when we think that we might have a few additional years on earth, most of us are taking more responsibility for our health and are continuing to make plans for the future with our loved ones.

God gave us time, He sat the moon and the sun in intervals that would help us regulate our lives and mark our years. Ever since, man has endeavored to understand and extend time by dividing the light and darkness into small and smaller intervals.

Scripture is careful to tell us that our time is not the same as God's time. Our finite minds could not accept the timeliness of God. He gave us only what we needed and could understand. But that has not swayed the human search for mastering time.

Aristotle viewed the present as something continually marching and changing in a linear motion. He described memories not as archives of our lives, but as tools. Only the fragments of an event linger in our minds to be consolidated into the construction of future events. By the year 160, the Roman emperor-philosopher Marcus Aurelius described time as a river of passing events. Moving in a specific direction at a consistent and measurable rate, from past to future. That is the concept that most of us have adopted through the years.

The most modern view of those efforts is that our concept of time is an individual one. That concept depends on Einstein's work in 1905 (Theory of Special Relativity) which established that the wristwatches of two observers in motion relative to one another will measure time differently. He posited that events don't happen in a set order. Time is not always segmented neatly into the past, the present and the future. Other scientists have explored the external and internal sensory inputs to define the perception of time as geography, location, orientation, language, writing, culture, and spatial metaphors.

ANCIENT CELTIC VIEW OF LIFE

Time is a circle, time goes round and round like a wheel, and that's why one hears echoes of the past continually – it's because the past is present, you don't have to look back down the straight line, you just look across the circle, and there are echoes of the past and the vision of the future and they're all present, all now, all forever. (Unknown)

"Everything comes to pass, nothing comes to stay except our loving faith."

ATTITUDE/GRATITUDE

Attitude is an adventure into the future: a conviction that everything will work together for our benefit. It is an extension of our faith that God is still working for us; He always comes through! We must learn to focus on the positive. That we don't automatically focus on the good is merely a bad habit. Change that habit for a better one: think positively in all things.

Gratitude is a renumeration of what has been granted to us in the past or present. Through no efforts of our own, we have survived and received adequate material wealth and the gift of spiritual satisfaction. We should be grateful for the good and the bad for our individual lives are the script that was written before the universe was created. Only the interference of our persistent free will can alter that script.

Attitude – forward hope; Gratitude – past blessings

Have you ever wondered why God has placed you here: in this generation – in this part of the universe and world – with these particular people? Of the 70-90 generations since the time of Jesus, why this cocoon of convenience and ease?

In my grandmother's memoir, she describes a weekly childhood task of washing the family's clothes in a mountain stream and pounding the clothes on a rock to dislodge the dirt. She then relays having to climb a steep hill back to the household clothesline to hang the wet clothes. In this day, I push a button, select a specific program, and walk away. My work is done! I do not deserve this comfort and assurance – saved time, more time – to do what?

More time to decide how to spend it? More time and more choices of what to do. Question, question, decision, decision…

Older people have a peculiar privilege: the chance to see God's faithfulness over time. Their troubles do not grow smaller as the years go by, but their multiple experiences can strengthen their confidence that God will deliver as he always has. (Psalm 71:18)

Paul told us what we need to know in 1 Cor. 15:1-4 and Acts 17:22-28. It is enough: Just the amount that we can understand. And mercifully, He gave us the Holy Spirit to help us in the individual details.

SPIRITUALITY

The condition of spirituality is an attitude toward life, responsibility, suffering – and death. It is a belief in self. It focuses on solving the meaning of life, and how people relate to each other. Spiritualists seek to answer questions about citizenship in the universe and other mysteries of human existence.

Spirituality can include deep feelings of connection to one's self, to relationships, to the community, and to God, fate, nature, or life in general. Spiritual experiences and individual concepts of spirituality are personal and vary from person to person. Spiritual belief can be founded on God, a specific religion, ethical principles, or humanistic values which we are all born with.

Some characteristics of a true spiritual person are:

lifelong psychological growth

creativity

consciousness and mindfulness

emotional maturation

thankfulness

appreciation

perceptivity

generosity

benevolence

awe and wonder of the world and universe

constant searching for life's meaning.

Many people use spirituality and religion as congruent terms, however, they are two very different attitudes to living a fruitful life.

Spirituality is the belief in the unique experiences of the self. Spiritual people can pick and choose their interpretation of life events. Usually, there is no one else who knows exactly what a spiritualist believes since everyone has a different ideology. Spiritualists primarily deal with the present moment; "it is what it is."

Religion is the belief in the experiences of others backed by secular history. Religious people seek to measure life events as prescribed through the stories of scripture and faith in the hidden purposes of God. Religious people are more oriented to the future "time here is short."

Spiritualists seek wisdom from life and believe that their experiences lead to knowledge and that the opportunity to use that knowledge increases wisdom. (experience + knowledge + opportunity = wisdom). Religious people seek knowledge first from scripture, leading to experience and opportunities to use events for the glory of God. (knowledge + experience + opportunity = wisdom).

More and more we hear that "I am not religious but spiritual." In this age, it is hard for most people to believe anything that cannot be explained by scientific evidence. As God allows us more and more subtle clues to the interchange of scripture, individualism, and history, faith is the supernatural component of the human mind that is being left out.

The beliefs of spirituality and religion can both serve as personal paths to better, more fruitful, and happier lives for our children. They both help all people to overcome stress, anxiety, poor health, and even the fear of death.

There are part-time spiritualists just as there are part-time Christians. It is likely harder for spiritualists to stay on an individual path because of the absence of a leader and the lack of a reference book. It is easier for a faltering spiritualist to be overlooked. Christians have the encouragement and the words of God to direct their way. As a member of a close-knit group, a struggling Christian is easily perceived and help is readily available.

The following comparisons are the belief of the true spiritualist and the anointed Christian as noted in literature:

Spiritualist	Christian
I seek the meaning of my life.	What purpose does God plan for me here?

I am a citizen of the universe.

I have a passport proving my citizenship in heaven.

I appreciate the opportunities in this world.

I appreciate the blessings of God given me in this world.

I am one with nature, I don't need temples or churches to worship.

I am one with God and worship Him everywhere.

I believe in a supreme being.

I believe in Jesus Christ and the Triune of God.

I expect a normal lifespan.

I expect to be taken up in The Rapture.

I do not utilize a life playbook.

I have a blueprint in scripture written before I was created.

I am in charge of my life.	The Lord is directing my life.
Everyone has a right to design his own life.	I am obligated to help others know Jesus.
There are many roads to heaven.	There is only one road to heaven, belief in Jesus.
Spirituality can be practiced individually and in private.	Religion is often practiced in a like-minded community.
My focus is on a personal journey of discovering my meaning.	My focus is a belief in God, religious texts, and traditions.
Christians and Muslims worship the same God.	Muslims do not worship Jesus and the triune of God.

Everyone has the right to make his own life decisions.	I respect the personal choices man makes even if he is wrong.
Can I be both spiritual and religious?	I can be a religious Christian spiritualist.

"Everything we do with and for the Lord is spiritual." Joyce Meyer, Bible teacher and author.

LOVE

Love is commonly considered an emotion or feeling, such as happiness, anger, or grief that can change in intensity. But love is a permanent psychological motivation such as hunger, thirst, sleep, and sex. (51) It is essential for human survival beginning in childhood and ending in the care of the dependent elder. Without appropriate love, at the prescribed time, human development can be thwarted, delayed, and perpetuated. Throughout life, love must be expanded and altered as stages of physical and psychological development evolve. Biology and society can determine how we think of love.

There are many types of love, including self-love, parental love, sibling love, spousal love and the love of God. These diverse types of love make it difficult to explain the phenomenon of love and the long-lasting consequences if the love is misinterpreted, abused or neglected.

Self love:

1. We are created in the image of God, but each of us is unique; there has never been a human being exactly like you. Your experiences, the people you have interacted with, and the personality you brought into the world have created the individual you are now.

2. You must love yourself before you can effectively enjoy the other types of love.

Parent love:

1. Parents are blessed with children but have a sacred charge of nourishing, protecting, and educating the child.

2. It is easy to love the little child, they are a part of you, an extension of yourself, and you look for and encourage signs of duplicity. Typically, the parent forgets that the child is "loaned not owned."

3. As the adolescent child begins to resent the stifling closeness, strife often develops between the child and the parent. Usually, that attitude lessens as the child ages into young adulthood – but not always.

4. Sometimes the adult child becomes estranged from the parent, becoming an adult seems harder than ever in our society. Ambitious parental expectations in a culture of comparison are keeping many young adults stuck in hostilities with their parents. (52). Experts report a growing trend of family estrangement among the young in the United States. Researchers find that 26 percent of young adults are estranged from their fathers, beginning, on average, at 23 years of age. A smaller number – 6 percent – are estranged from their mother. Cutting off contact with parents is, however surprising, a way of resetting the parental relationship. (53)

Sibling love:

In childhood, brothers and sisters compete for parental attention and love, which can last throughout life. "She always loved her best." Sibling placement in the family can determine expectations. Recent studies indicate that the oldest child in the family is not necessarily the leader despite traditional thinking. Only a slight IQ advantage has been proven to exist in the first child of a family. Parents often make choices of guidance based on an erroneous assessment of the needs of each child.

Jesus reminded us that everyone is a brother and sister to us and equally loved. In later years, siblings often become confidants. "She is the only one who knew me as a child." "We talk of episodes in our lives that we interpreted differently both then and now."

Spousal love:

There is a time in human development when cultural, psychological, and physical expectations encourage falling in love. When a person meets another who matches a preconceived idea of love, a relationship and possible marriage develop.

Dr. Zick Rubin, an American social psychologist (54) writes that there are three elements of love:

1. Attachment - needing to be cared for and be with the other person. Physical contact and approval are also important components of attachment.

2. Caring – valuing the other person's happiness and needs as much as your own.

3. Intimacy – sharing your private thoughts, feelings, and desires with the other person.

Scripture reveals to us the importance that God placed on marriage between a man and a woman. Love is mentioned 686 times in the Bible (NIV).

There are many new theories of how to describe love, but we have a prescription that has always been there for us in 1 Cor. 13:3.

Love is:

patient

kind

does not envy

does not boast

Is not proud

Is not rude

Is not self-seeking

Is not easily angered

keeps no record of wrongs

does not delight in evil

rejoices in truth

always protects

always trusts

always hopes

always perseveres

Spousal love is a oneness that anticipates the needs of another and puts those needs before those of our own. It is an enduring partnership with the goal of establishing a satisfying and suitable home for the possible blessing of children.

God's love:

The love of God passeth all understanding and is exemplified in the cross of Christ. That love never fails.

CONCLUSIONS

No one wants to get old, lose independence, or become ill. But remember, we were born into the world with a promise that the Lord would bless and support believers for ?? number of days on earth. Placement here is only temporary. Your present home cannot be compared to your heavenly home where your permanent citizenship resides forever.

In this waiting period, enjoy the world and situation where you are placed. Seek the purpose of your brief stay. Sing, dance, work and worship with joy and thanksgiving for the opportunity!

"None of us want to fade away without having made our mark on the landscape." (55)

EXPERT REFERENCES

1. Raphelson, Samantha. October 6, 2014. NTR National Public Radio.

2. Wikipedia. The Free Encyclopedia. Maximum Lifespan.

3. Dyer, Wayne and Dee Garnes. 2015. Memories of Heaven. Hay House, Inc.

4. Stefanacci, Richard G. Overview of Aging. Thomas Jefferson University, Jefferson College of Population Health.

5. Health Issues. Why the color of our eyes can change as we age. March 2024.

6. AARP The Magazine/Real Possibilities, June/July 2020.

7. AARP The Magazine/Real Possibilities, June 1/July 2020.

8. www.cybersalt.org/clean-jokes/ancestery.

9. Piper, John. Rethinking Retirement: Finishing Life for the Glory of Christ. Crossway Publishing. 2009.

10. "Your Guide to a Happy Healthy Life". Better Homes & Gardens, November 2019.

11. O'Leary, Patrick. The poem "Nobody Knows It But Me". General Motors Commercial. 2002.

12. Jeremiah, David. Sanctuary, finding moments of refuge in the presence of God. Integrity Publisher, Nashville, Tenn. 2002. Page 291.

13. Darling, Lynn. AARP The Magazine/Real Possibilities. "Is there a Cure for Loneliness? December 2019/January 2020.

14. Winch, Guy. "Solutions for the Solitary", Psychology Today, July/August/2017.

15. Porter, Andrew. Short Story: The Letters. Texas Monthly, February, 2024.

16. Rohn, Jim. https://www.success.com/article/ rohn-4 tips-for setting-powerful-goals. 2017.

17. Rice, Joyce. Think it! Work It! Do It! Winning in Life and Business. 2019.

18. Finkel, Michael. Want to Fall Asleep? Read This Story. National Geographic, August, 2018.

19. Zaddra, Antonio and Robert Stickgold. Theater of the Mind. Psychology Today, January/February, 2021.

20. Butler,Kathrine Anne. The Art of Dying Well. Scribner, New York, NY. 2019.

21. Arthur, Alua. A Guiding Light at the End of Life. Psychology Today, June, 2024.

22. Burke, John. Imagine heaven & Imagine the God of heaven. Baker Books and Tyndale House. 2015 & 2023.

23. Boone, Peggy & Bonnie Headington. Our Walk With Elephants. Publish America, Baltimore. 2003.

24. https://www.cdc.gov/suicide/facts/data.

25. Boone, Peggy & Bonnie Headington. Our Walk With Elephants. Publish America, Baltimore. 2003.

26. https://www.goodreads.com/quotes/1340624.

27. https://twisted.sifter/2014/02/if -the- world- were- only-100- people/

28. American Psychological Association. November 28, 2005.

29. Uklomogbe, Juliane. Where Are Emotions Felt in the Body? Greatist, September 9, 2020.

30. Poscente, Vince. The Ant and the Elephant. Libretto Publishing. 2006.

31. https://www.mayoclinic.org./diseases-condi-cions/arthritis/2035077. August 29, 2023.

32. Globocan 2022: Latest global cancer data shows rising incidence and stark inequities. https://www.uicc.org/news/globocan.

33. https://www.bing.com. Overactive bladder treatment/ Over active bladder symptoms?

34. Healthline. https://www./bing.com

35. McArthur, John. Why bad things happen to good people. New Testament Commentary on 2 Corinthians.

36. Marquis, Arthur. Why do some people have a higher pain tolerance than others? Health Magazine, March 26, 2024.

37. Woods, Geoff and Ya-Chun Chen. Explainer: why don't some people feel pain? The Conversation. October 20,

38. https://www.pet-ownership/do-dogs-go-to-heaven.

39. https://www.wiseoldsaying.com/grandchildren-quotes/

40. Encyclopedia Britannica. Weather forecasting. 20 December, 2023.

41. Johnson, Matt. Why We Love Sports. Mind, Brain, and Value, August 25, 2020.

42. https://www.keepbelieving.com/sermon/forgiveness-healing-the-hurt-we -never-deserved/

43. https://www.bing.com/searching?q=forgiveness.

44. Pipher, Mary. Women Rowing North. Bloomsbury Publisher, 1385 Broadway, NY. 2019.

45. Colapinto, John. The Extraordinary World of Music. AARP Magazine December 2023/ January 2024.

46. Slepian, Michael. The Secret Life of Secrets. Crown Publishing. June 7, 2022.

47. National Institute on Aging. https://www.nih. gov/health/mental/and emotional-health-de- pression-and-older adults.

48. Burns, David. Feeling Good: The New Mood Therapy. William Morrow & Company. NY, 1980; Avon. 1992.

49. https://www.emotionalcompetency.com/ shame.htm.

50. https://www.goodreads.com/quotes/95085.

51. Burunat, Enriques. Love is a physiological motivation (like hunger, thirst, sleep or sex).

Med Hypothesis, August, 2019. Elsevier Ltd. 129:109225.

52. PT Contributions. Growing All The Way Up. Psychology Today/ January/February. 2024.

53. Marano, Hara Estroff. The Pain of Cut-Offs. Psychology Today/ January-February, 2024.

54. Rubin, Zick. Rubin's Elements of Love. Verywellmind.com.

55. Watkins, Joe. Storied Rock. National Geographic. May, 2024.

ATTACHMENT

Prayer For The Aged

"Lord, Thou knowest better than I know myself that I am growing older, and will someday be old.

"Keep me from getting talkative, and particularly from the fatal habit of thinking I must say something on every occasion.

"Release me from craving to try to straighten out everybody's affairs.

"Keep my mind free from the recital of endless details – give me wings to get to the point.

"I ask for grace enough to listen to the tales of others' pains. Please help me to endure them with patience.

"But seal my lips on my own aches and pains – they are increasing and my love of rehearsing them is becoming sweeter as the years go by.

"Teach me the glorious lesson that occasionally it is possible that I may be mistaken.

"Keep me reasonably sweet; I do not want to be a saint – some of them are so hard to live with – but a sour old person is one of the crowning works of the devil.

"Make me thoughtful, but not moody; helpful, but not bossy. With my vast store of wisdom, it seems a pity not to use it all – but Thou knowest, Lord, that I want a few friends at the end."

Author Unknown

Great Expectations of Aging

Book II

Caretaking

Choices

Commitment

Control

Friends

Intuition

Joy

Legacy

 # 1

Gender

Marriage

Parenting

www.ingramcontent.com/pod-product-compliance
Lightning Source LLC
Chambersburg PA
CBHW021137260726
48656CB00023B/170